WRITERS AND THEIR WORK

Isobel Armstrong

H46 059 658 2

Please renew/return this item by the last date shown.

From Area codes 01923 or 020:	From Area codes of Herts:
Renewals: 01923 471373	01438 737373
Enquiries: 01923 471333	01438 737333
Textphone: 01923 471599	01438 737599

www.hertsdirect.org/librarycatalogue

ELIZABETH BARRETT BROWNING

Simon Avery

NORTHCOTE

BRITISH
COUNCIL

© Copyright 2011 by Simon Avery

First published in 2011 by Northcote House Publishers Ltd, Horndon, Tavistock, Devon, PL19 9NQ, United Kingdom.
Tel: +44 (0) 1822 810066 Fax: +44 (0) 1822 810034.

British Library Cataloguing-in-Publication Data
A catalogue record for this book is available from the British Library

ISBN 978-0-7463-1201-8 hardcover
ISBN 978-0-7463-1206-3 paperback

Typeset by PDQ Typesetting, Newcastle-under-Lyme
Printed and bound in the United Kingdom

For Pat Wheeler,
a true friend

Contents

Acknowledgements

There are many people who have been involved in the production of this book and I am glad to be able to have the opportunity to thank them here.

Firstly, I would like to thank Isobel Armstrong and Brian Hulme for giving me the opportunity to write the book in the first instance and for their patience with deadlines when I took up a new teaching post. I would also like to thank my colleagues in the Department of English, Linguistics and Cultural Studies at the University of Westminster for their support throughout the writing period, and particularly Alex Warwick who enabled me to have the space for research which was necessary to bring the project to fruition.

During the years that I have been working on Elizabeth Barrett Browning, I have had the opportunity to meet, work and make friends with some wonderful scholars and I would like to thank them formally here for their generosity with both time and knowledge. I would particularly like to thank Alison Chapman, Berry Chevasco, Sandra Donaldson, Rowena Fowler, Vicky Greenaway, Cora Kaplan, Scott Lewis, Tricia Lootens, Jennifer McDonell, Michael Meredith, Barbara Neri, Pamela Neville-Sington, Joe Phelan, Marjorie Stone, Rebecca Stott and Beverley Taylor. Thanks are also due to Elizabeth Woodworth, who kindly read and offered invaluable suggestions on initial drafts of this book, and to the reader for Northcote House, who provided extremely useful comments on the final version.

Many friends have offered support in various ways and I would like say a big thank you to Catherine Carey, Carrie Etter, Monica Germanà, Vicky Griffin, Anna Holyland, Rowland Hughes, Matt Morrison, Patrick O'Malley, Anita Pacheco, Imogen Rogers, Louisa Summer, Pat Wheeler and Anne Witchard. Love and thanks as always to my parents, Nina and Mike Avery, who have lived with Barrett Browning for longer than I care to remember, and to Steven Little who has been there throughout the whole process with constant support and encouragement.

Biographical Outline

1806	Elizabeth Barrett Moulton-Barrett (EBB) born at Coxhoe Hall, County Durham, on 6 March, the eldest of the twelve children of Edward Moulton-Barrett (1785–1857) and Mary Graham Clarke (1781–1828). (One of the children, Mary, dies in infancy.)
1809	The Barrett family moves to Hope End, near Ledbury in Herefordshire, a large estate where Edward Barrett builds a mansion in the Regency Gothic style.
1812	Robert Browning (RB) born on 7 May in Camberwell, south London.
1815	October to November: EBB and her parents travel round France, visiting Paris, Rouen and Boulogne.
1820	*The Battle of Marathon* privately printed by EBB's father for her birthday.
1820–1	EBB writes 'Glimpses into My Own Life and Literary Character', an important autobiographical essay.
1821	EBB's illness, which is undefined at this point, begins. Her first officially published poems, written about Greece, are published in *The New Monthly Magazine*.
1824	'Stanzas on the Death of Lord Byron' published in *The Globe and Traveller*.
1826	*An Essay on Mind, and Other Poems* published. It initiates EBB's friendships with the classical scholars, Uvedale Price and Hugh Stuart Boyd.
1828	EBB's mother dies in July.
1831–2	EBB keeps a diary (extant), detailing her intellectual development, anxieties about her family, and her complex feelings about Hugh Stuart Boyd.
1832	Following the emancipation of slaves on the plantations in Jamaica – from which the Barrett family wealth is derived – Edward Barrett is forced to sell

	Hope End. The family initially moves to Sidmouth.
1833	*Prometheus Bound, Translated from the Greek of Æschylus, and Miscellaneous Poems* published.
1835	The Barretts move to Gloucester Place, London, in December.
1836	In May, John Kenyon, EBB's distant cousin, introduces EBB to Mary Russell Mitford, subsequently a close friend. She also meets Wordsworth at a dinner party at Kenyon's house.
1837	EBB begins writing for Mitford's annual, *Findens' Tableaux*.
1838	In April, the Barretts move to 50 Wimpole Street. *The Seraphim, and Other Poems* published, the first volume to appear under EBB's own name. In August, EBB moves to Torquay on her doctor's recommendation, where she stays until September 1841.
1840	EBB's adored brother, Edward, who has come to stay with his sister, is drowned on 11 July whilst sailing in Tor Bay. EBB is ill from grief and guilt for months afterwards.
1841	EBB moves back to London in September.
1842	EBB's critical work, *Some Account of the Greek Christian Poets*, is published in the *Athenaeum*. This is followed three months later by *The Book of Poets*, a series of essays on the history of poetry.
1844	*Poems* (2 volumes) published (the title of the American edition is *A Drama of Exile, and Other Poems*). It is EBB's most acclaimed collection to date.
1845	Having read the reference to his work in 'Lady Geraldine's Courtship' (*Poems*, 1844), RB writes to EBB on 10 January, initiating the relationship which will lead to their marriage. RB first visits EBB at Wimpole Street on 20 May. In August, EBB starts writing the poems which will become *Sonnets from the Portuguese*.
1846	EBB and RB are secretly married on 12 September at Marylebone Church (EBB's father has forbidden any of his children to marry). A week later they leave for the Continent, travelling first to Paris and then to Pisa. On the way, EBB receives a letter from her father disowning her.

1847	In April, the Brownings move to Florence and, in July, rent rooms in Casa Guidi. On 12 September, their first anniversary, a major procession takes place outside their apartment, celebrating Grand Duke Leopold of Tuscany's granting the Florentines a civic guard. This will become the basis for Part One of EBB's *Casa Guidi Windows*. In December, 'The Runaway Slave at Pilgrim's Point' is published in the Boston anti-slavery annual, *The Liberty Bell* (1848 edition).
1849	The Brownings' son, Robert Wiedemann ('Penini'), born on 9 March. In July, EBB gives RB the sequence of sonnets which will be published as *Sonnets from the Portuguese*. RB's *Poems* published.
1850	*Poems*, an expanded and revised edition of *Poems* (1844) including 'Runaway Slave' and *Sonnets from the Portuguese*, published. In June, following the death of Wordsworth, EBB is proposed for the post of Poet Laureate by the *Athenaeum*. RB publishes *Christmas-Eve and Easter-Day*.
1851	*Casa Guidi Windows* published. The Brownings spend the year travelling around Europe, including London where they see family and visit the Great Exhibition. In October, they move into lodgings on the Champs-Elysées in Paris.
1852	In February, EBB meets George Sand twice. In July, the Brownings travel to London, returning to Paris two months later. In October, they watch Louis Napoleon's triumphant entry into Paris. They return to Florence in November.
1853	The Brownings stay at Bagni di Lucca from July to October and then travel to Rome where they stay until mid-1854, before returning to Florence.
1855	RB's *Men and Women* published. In July, the Brownings travel to London and then, in October, to Paris where they stay until June 1856.
1856	*Aurora Leigh* published in November (the second impression is published in January 1857 and the third in March).

John Kenyon dies, leaving the Brownings enough money to make them financially secure.

Revised edition of *Poems* published.

1857 EBB's father dies in April. He and EBB have never been reconciled.

1858 The Brownings stay in Paris from July to October and then move to Rome in November where they stay until May 1859.

1859 EBB's health starts to deteriorate during the summer, at the same time as she loses hope for the success of the *Risorgimento*. In July, the Brownings travel to Siena, returning to Florence in October. In November, they leave for Rome for the winter.

1860 *Poems Before Congress* published.

In June, the Brownings return to Florence. In July, they travel to Siena where they stay until November, before they move to Rome.

In December, EBB's sister, Henrietta, dies from cancer.

1861 In June, the Brownings return to Florence. EBB's health deteriorates and she dies on 30 June in Robert's arms. On 1 July she is buried in Florence's Protestant Cemetery.

RB and Pen leave for London in August; RB never returns to Florence.

1862 *Last Poems* published in March.

In October, the Florentine council erects a plaque on Casa Guidi celebrating EBB's contribution to Italian unification.

Abbreviations and References

It is now becoming more usual in critical work on Elizabeth Barrett Browning to abbreviate her name to EBB. This is because of the difficulty of constantly switching accurately between her family name, Elizabeth Barrett Barrett, and her more familiar married name, Elizabeth Barrett Browning. I have followed the convention of using EBB throughout this study.

Just as I began work on the proofs of this book, the long-awaited *Works of Elizabeth Barrett Browning* was published by Pickering and Chatto (5 volumes, 2010). This text has been years in the making and has drawn upon the hard work and expertise of an international team of EBB scholars – including Marjorie Stone, Beverly Taylor, Rita Patterson, Cynthia Burgess, Clara Drummond, Barbara Neri, Elizabeth Woodworth and Jane Stewart Laux – under the general editorship of Sandra Donaldson. It is a momentous publication and offers the first complete edition of EBB's writings since Charlotte Porter and Helen A. Clarke's 1900 edition, a version that was problematic in a number of ways. The new *Works* reprints all EBB's published writings, with headnotes and annotations, and also includes over five hundred pages of poems, translations and prose fragments which were unpublished during EBB's lifetime, many of them having been taken from manuscript sources.

Without doubt, *The Works of Elizabeth Barrett Browning* is now the definitive edition for EBB scholars and I am grateful to my copyeditor, Katie Ryde, for allowing me, at a very late stage, to change all the references in this critical study so that they align with the new edition.

The following abbreviations are used throughout:

Correspondence   *The Brownings' Correspondence*, ed. Philip Kelley,
                       Ronald Hudson and Scott Lewis, 16 vols

	(Winfield, KS: Wedgestone Press, 1984–)
Works	*The Works of Elizabeth Barrett Browning*, ed. Sandra Donaldson *et al.*, 5 vols (London: Pickering and Chatto, 2010)
Ogilvy	*Elizabeth Barrett Browning's Letters to Mrs David Ogilvy, 1849–1861*, ed. Peter N. Heydon and Philip Kelley (London: John Murray, 1974)
Mitford	*The Letters of Elizabeth Barrett Browning to Mary Russell Mitford, 1836–1854*, ed. Meredith B. Raymond and Mary Rose Sullivan, 3 vols (Winfield, KS: Armstrong Browning Library and Wedgestone Press, 1983)

Preface

The original *Writers and their Work* volume on Elizabeth Barrett Browning, written by the key EBB critic of the period, Alethea Hayter, was published in 1965. Only 29 pages in length and drawing upon some of the insights developed in Hayter's earlier book-length study, *Mrs Browning: A Poet's Work and Its Setting* (1962), the *Writers and their Work* volume offered a swift overview of EBB's career and some specific points on language and prosody, before closing with a telling assessment of the perceived status of EBB's poetry at that time:

> Her poetry is very much out of favour with the academic critics and historians of literature. You will not find it among the set books in British university courses in English literature, nor in the latest anthologies.... No edition of the collected works is in print in Britain... [and her] memory is kept alive at present more by the unending series of plays, films and musical comedies concerned with her private life than by readers of her poetry.
>
> It is still too soon to say whether her fame as a poet will ever return. She may have to wait two hundred years, as Ford and Webster did till Charles Lamb brought them back to life.[1]

Interestingly, Hayter's phrasing here recalls Virginia Woolf's humorous but poignant assessment of EBB in her 1931 essay on *Aurora Leigh*:

> fate has not been kind to Mrs Browning as a writer. Nobody reads her, nobody discusses her, nobody troubles to put her in her place. ... In short, the only place in the mansion of literature that is assigned her is downstairs in the servants' quarters, where, in company with Mrs Hemans, Eliza Cook, Jean Ingelow, Alexander Smith, Edwin Arnold, and Robert Montgomery, she bangs the crockery about and eats vast handfuls of peas on the point of her knife.[2]

In the three decades between Woolf and Hayter's analyses, then, little seemed to have shifted. EBB, the once internationally-renowned and highly-influential poet, had been firmly pushed to the margins of literary history, her status as writer of some of the most powerful and innovative poetic works of the nineteenth century erased by both the general modernist backlash against Victorian literature and the processes of early twentieth-century canon formation. It is a fascinating history, which has been carefully detailed by Marjorie Stone and Tricia Lootens, and it has much to tell us about the shifting notions of literary value and critical debate. For the poet who, at her death, was celebrated by the Florentine council for her role in bringing about Italian unification and who was lauded by many major figures of the Victorian literary world was, by the middle of the following century, all but lost from view, reduced to the ailing heroine of one of literary history's most famous romances and the writer of one of the most reproduced poetic lines ever: 'How do I love thee? Let me count the ways' (*Sonnets from the Portuguese*, sonnet 43, l.1).[3]

But then, as Margaret Reynolds notes in her mapping of the history of EBB criticism, 'feminism happened' and EBB studies entered a whole new phase.[4] For in 1979, *Aurora Leigh* was republished for the first time in seven decades, edited by the Marxist-feminist scholar Cora Kaplan and released by the Women's Press. The poem was quickly taken up in feminist academic circles since, as Lorna Sage wrote in her review of the edition, here was 'a poem so well-equipped for time-travel' and one which clearly spoke to the second-wave feminist movement.[5] Three decades later, *Aurora Leigh* continues to speak to us in multiple and diverse ways. Indeed, the poem which scholars generally agree to be EBB's most significant work (as EBB herself did) has subsequently become one of the most critically-examined and discussed works of Victorian poetry in general and certainly, along with Christina Rossetti's *Goblin Market* (1862), one of the most widely-debated works by a Victorian woman poet.

Since the mid-1980s – and particularly since the sustained and expansive recovery of Victorian women's poetry to which EBB has been central – concern with *Aurora Leigh* has led to consideration of EBB's other diverse writings: her ballads, dramatic monologues, religious poetry and nature poetry; her socio-political works on industrialization, slavery and the Italian *Risorgimento*; her prose works, letters and essays; and, more recently, the juvenilia which is often more innovative and incisive than has been previously acknowledged. Articles and monographs on EBB are appearing far more regularly, her voluminous correspondence continues to be published, new editions of her poetry are appearing, and international conferences on all aspects of her work are being held. Without doubt, EBB is back, having escaped the basement in the mansion of literature assigned to her by Woolf and proving herself to be both one of the most complex and challenging poets of her day and highly relevant to our own given her concerns with gender relations, the shaping and manipulation of power, national and international politics, and consideration of what might constitute a meaningful existence. Certainly, hers is one of the success stories of modern criticism and its attendant rethinking of the established canon.

In this study I have sought to take a line through EBB's poetry which is particularly concerned with the search for a 'home'. In July 2007, I was given the opportunity to talk on EBB at the Ledbury Poetry Festival as part of an event held at Hope End, EBB's home during her youth.[6] This led me to a concern with how 'home' is represented in her work, for EBB's poetry is populated with protagonists and speakers who are constantly searching for a place of security within what Romney Leigh terms 'this loud-transition time' (*Aurora Leigh* 4:343). This place of security is defined in various and multiple ways and I have used this as the structuring principle for this book. In Chapter 1, I explore EBB's poetics across her career overall and particularly her own search for a 'home' in relation to inherited poetic traditions and thinking on the role of the poet. In Chapter 2, I examine her religious poetry in more detail and consider how the speakers and protagonists in a number of her poems undertake a search for a spiritual home with Christ or God. This is paralleled by the concern in Chapter 3 with those poems which consider the search for a secure home in the *temporal* world, engendered by love and meaningful human relations. Then, in Chapter 4, I focus on those poems which see EBB's speakers and protagonists searching for the security of a *political* home, defined in terms of liberal politics and the establishment of a nation state which is supportive and secure for all its citizens.

As will become evident fairly rapidly, however, this search for a home by EBB's poetic figures is often highly problematic and ultimately illusory and unfulfilled. Indeed, in Chapter 5, I argue that it is only in the long, discursive *Aurora Leigh* that a secure home is finally attainable, where the religious, emotional and political elements are all present and interconnected. Yet as the Conclusion to this study suggests, the poems which EBB wrote after *Aurora Leigh* – she would live for another five years – return once more to the notion of a fragmented and unattainable home and a concern with the exile in the modern world. Indeed, the notion of home as a place of security appears to remain an ideal in EBB's poetry as a whole and one which it is impossible to engender except under very particular circumstances.

Within this framework, I have considered a range of both EBB's more familiar poems, such as *Aurora Leigh*, 'A Romance of the Ganges', 'The Cry of the Children' and 'The Runaway Slave at Pilgrim's Point', and less well-known but intriguing works such as *The Seraphim*, *A Drama of Exile*, 'An Island' and 'On a Portrait of Wordsworth by B. R. Haydon'. For reasons of space, I have obviously had to prioritize particular poems over others. Consequently, where I have dealt with longer poems in detail in previous critical work – as is the case with *The Battle of Marathon*, *An Essay on Mind*, and, especially, *Casa Guidi Windows* – I have only given limited attention to them here. Similarly, where I have not had space to analyse larger texts in depth, as is the case with the *Sonnets from the Portuguese*, I have indicated where readers can find additional critical material on them.

1

The Shaping of a Poetics

> Poetry has been as serious a thing to me as life itself; and
> life has been a very serious thing: there has been no
> playing at skittles for me in either. I never mistook
> pleasure for the final cause of poetry; nor leisure, for the
> hour of the poet. I have done my work, so far, as
> work...and as work I offer it to the public...
>
> (*Works* 2:570)

Thus wrote Elizabeth Barrett in the preface to her fourth
collection of poetry, the two-volume *Poems* published in 1844. By
this stage, EBB was a well-established poet with a growing
reputation and, as this phrasing suggests, a poet who was
dedicated to her craft as intellectual labour requiring skill and
determination. The writing of poetry was neither a game nor an
accomplishment for her but a demanding and challenging
profession. Indeed, six years after the publication of *Poems*,
EBB's commitment to her 'work' would result in her being put
forward for the post of poet laureate on the death of William
Wordsworth in 1850. It would be, the *Athenaeum* argued, 'an
honourable testimonial to the individual' and 'a fitting recogni-
tion of the remarkable place which the women of England have
taken in the literature of the day.'[1] EBB is one of very few
women to have been seriously considered for the laureateship –
which was only awarded to a female poet, Carol Ann Duffy, for
the first time in 2009 – and whilst the 1850 post was eventually
awarded to Alfred Tennyson, the debate about EBB as potential
laureate reveals how she had firmly claimed a position in the
public consciousness as one of Britain's leading poetic figures,
despite the fact that by then she was living as an expatriate poet
in Florence.

But what did EBB consider the function of the poet to be?
How did she think the poet was formed? And what currency did

1

she believe poetry to have in the modern world? In both her poems and prose writings (her prefaces, essays and letters), EBB is constantly grappling with these questions and interrogating her profession throughout a career which spans five decades from the mid-Romantic period to the mid-Victorian period. In this chapter, then, I explore some of these writings in order to tease out EBB's changing sense of her role as she shaped and refashioned her poetics throughout her lifetime. In particular, I pay attention to the extensive number of poems which she composed *about* poets (both generic poets and specific writers) as a means of locating a 'home' for her work in relation to established poetic traditions on the one hand and new modern contexts on the other. It was this continual examination of her vocation, I argue, which was fundamental to EBB's transformation into one of the period's major writers.

EBB's determination to become a poet and her exploration of the role of poetry in society began remarkably early, at Hope End, the Barrett family home in Herefordshire where she lived from 1809 to 1832. As she reveals in her early autobiographical essay, 'Glimpses into My Own Life and Literary Character' (1820–1), she was dedicated to authorship from a young age and encouraged in her literary ambitions by her parents. In an oft-quoted passage, for example, she records how her future vocation was all but established by her father's acknowledgment of her abilities: 'for some lines on virtue which I had pen[n]ed with great care I received from Papa a ten shilling note enclosed in a letter which was addrest to *the Poet Laureat* [*sic*] *of Hope End*; I mention this because I received much more pleasure from the word *Poet* than from the ten shilling note' (*Correspondence* 1:350). This is a remarkable title to be offered to the girl who, three decades later, would be proposed for the actual laureateship and the young EBB immediately sought to lay claim to the position. For as both 'Glimpses' and EBB's voluminous extant correspondence make clear, from this point onwards EBB pursued her desired career with a commitment which is astonishing for its unwavering single-mindedness.

Central to this commitment was reading as a means of intellectual expansion and from the earliest age EBB read widely and liberally. By the age of seven, she notes in 'Glimpses', she was already seeking to 'form my taste . . . to see what was best to write about & read about' (*Correspondence* 1:350) and she subsequently studied Shakespeare, Milton, translations of the *Iliad* and *Odyssey*, and histories of England, Greece and Rome. This was the start of a lifelong concern with self-education which, twenty years later, would be reflected in the title work of EBB's first major collection, *An Essay on Mind, and Other Poems* (1826). Written in the style of Alexander Pope's 'verse essays', *An Essay on Mind* is a long philosophical poem in which EBB examines the nature of genius, that 'Prometheus of our earth' (l.121) as she terms it, as it is manifested in the work of philosophers, scientists, historians and poets. The level of engagement with scores of (exclusively male) intellectuals is astonishing as EBB summarizes and judges the contributions made to the advancement of knowledge by thinkers as historically and culturally diverse as Homer, Plato, Archimedes, Dante, Petrarch, Shakespeare, Bacon, Kepler, Newton, Locke, Hobbes, Racine, Paine and Byron. Significantly, part of EBB's agenda in the poem is to emphasize the need to make connections between ideas, to see concepts holistically and to avoid becoming trapped in details or partial views: 'For Mind is narrow'd, not inspir'd by parts', she asserts (l.1011). Further, she argues that individuals need to think *actively* and not simply accept inherited wisdoms without question.[2] Both these concerns – the need to synthesize ideas and the need to challenge established lines of thinking – are ones which EBB promoted throughout her career and ones which, *An Essay on Mind* and subsequent poems suggest, poets are best able to uphold.

'My time is continually engaged either in writing,' EBB would reflect in 1828, 'or in reading that I *may write*' (*Correspondence* 2:105). Increasingly, this reading would be undertaken not only in English but also in a range of modern and ancient languages, including French, German, Spanish, Italian, Hebrew, Latin and Greek. Amongst these, EBB's commitment to Latin and Greek is especially significant given that in the eighteenth and nineteenth centuries an education in the classics was usually considered a prerequisite for a (male) poet. Greek had a particular interest for EBB (she was far less drawn to Latin) and she pursued her studies tirelessly from the age of eleven. As she wrote in 'Glimpses', once she had made up her mind to be 'considered an authoress', she 'felt the most ardent desire to understand the learned languages – To comprehend even the Greek alphabet was delight inexpressible' (*Correspondence* 1:350). Despite the fact that the classics were firmly considered to be male intellectual terrain – as Rowena Fowler notes, classical study was associated with the transition to manhood and entrance into university, the law, the church and the civil service[3] – EBB was initially encouraged by her father, who allowed her to work alongside her brother Edward under the guidance of his tutor. Even when Edward was sent to Charterhouse in 1820, EBB resolutely continued her classical learning on her own until, following the publication of *An Essay on Mind* in 1826, she was contacted independently by two renowned classical scholars who had read and admired her poetry: Sir Uvedale Price, who was eighty at the time of first writing and with whom EBB maintained an energetic correspondence on classical literature until his death in 1829; and the blind scholar and poet Hugh Stuart Boyd (1781–1848), who offered EBB what was arguably her most important intellectual relationship before her meeting with Robert Browning in the 1840s. Over the next eight years, until the Barrett family left Hope End, EBB corresponded with and visited Boyd on a regular basis, enabling her to expand her knowledge of classical works to a phenomenal degree. For even a cursory examination of EBB's letters of the period reveals her detailed knowledge of the works of Aristotle, Cicero, Euripides, Hesiod, Homer, Horace, Juvenal, Livy, Pindar, Pliny, Sallust, Theocritus and Virgil – an astonishing education by any account. Certainly for EBB the study of the classics and the profession of poet were firmly intertwined, as she indicated to Boyd in 1827: 'I intend to give up *Greek*, when I give up *poetry*: & ... *not till then*' (*Correspondence* 2:56).

The greatest influence on EBB's thinking about her vocation and the shaping of her poetics, however, was her reading of other established poets. As Marjorie Stone has emphasized, EBB was acutely aware of her contemporaneousness or near-contemporaneousness with the great Romantic poets,[4] and it is in relation to three of these that I want to locate EBB's emerging sense of herself as poet. The first is an author who, until recently, has lain on the margins of the canon of Romantic poetry and whose influence on EBB's concept of the poet appears to have remained unexplored: James Beattie (1735–1803). As EBB notes in 'Glimpses', it was Beattie's poem *The Minstrel*, published in two books in 1771 and 1774, that first fired her love of poetry:

> I think the story [i.e. prose] interested me more tha[n] the poetry till 'The Minstrel' met my sight...The brilliant imagery[,] the fine metaphors and the flowing numbers...truly astonished me. Every stanza excited my ardent admiration nor can I now remember the delight which I felt on perusing those pages without enthusiasm – (*Correspondence* 1:350)

Written in Spenserian stanzas, a form which EBB herself experimented with in 'Spenserian Stanzas: On a Boy of Three Years Old' (1826), *The Minstrel* is an early *künstlerroman*, one of the first sustained attempts to trace the growth of a poet's mind and therefore an important precursor of, and model for, those more well-known Romantic auto/biographies, Wordsworth's *Excursion* (1814) and *Prelude* (1850), Byron's *Childe Harold's Pilgrimage* (1812–18), Shelley's *Alastor* (1816) and Keats' *Endymion* (1818). Subtitled 'The Progress of Genius', the poem focuses on the development of Edwin, the son of a shepherd who passes his youth either exploring the sublime landscape of his Scottish homeland or absorbed in reading and local oral narratives. Constantly hastening away to places 'remote from man' (Book 1, l.291),[5] he constitutes an early version of both the Romantic wanderer figure and the divinely-inspired visionary, with nature and imagination central to his subject formation. In the second book of the poem, however, this naïve otherworldliness is shattered when Edwin encounters an enigmatic hermit who forces him to realise that the world is founded upon brutal power structures, tyranny and violence, and that by ignoring this and retreating into the imagination too far the poet would be caught in a barren psychological space, 'a dark waste, where fiends and tempests howl' (Book 2, l.413). What the poem suggests, therefore, is the need to balance commitment to imagination and nature with a wider understanding of philosophy, politics, science and the materialities of the social world. The 'comprehensive mind' (2:487) created by this amalgam of concerns would then enable the poet, Beattie suggests, to bring about transformative change in society, which is envisaged here in terms of challenging oppressive socio-political structures, unifying a nation, and ushering in a better world – ideas which interestingly prefigure many of EBB's own later concerns. Through this process, the minstrel would be able to move from the margins of society to the centre, 'mindful of the aids that life requires,/ And of the services man owes to man' (2:507–8).

As critics such as Joseph Bristow, Alan Sinfield and Carol T. Christ have argued, this notion of where poetry is placed in relation to society is crucial to discussions regarding the function of poetic writings and the construction of the poet during both the Romantic and Victorian periods.[6] Is the poet important to the exploration of socio-political concerns and therefore at the centre of the community? Or is poetry an increasingly irrelevant art form in a world dominated by industrialization, utilitarianism and the loss of totalising belief systems? These were debates to which EBB would constantly return and whilst *The Minstrel* might offer something of a fictionalized resolution of these tensions, it was rather the literary lives of two of the great male Romantic poets which most evidently shaped EBB's own position.

The first of these poets was William Wordsworth (1770–1850), whose *Lyrical Ballads* (1798), with its important 'Preface' asserting poetry's status as 'the breath and finer spirit of all knowledge', articulated a new kind of aesthetic manifesto.[7] For in his celebration of nature as benevolent nurturing spirit and moral teacher – a position which, Jerome McGann argues, developed partly in reaction to the horrors of industrialization and the loss of political idealism[8] – and in his focus on an array of outcast and dispossessed figures such as 'The Idiot Boy', 'The Mad Mother' and 'The Leech-Gatherer', Wordsworth broke new ground in ways which were distinctly anti-metropolitan and which called for a rethinking of the everyday through processes of defamiliarization. Moreover, like many of the other Romantic poets, Wordsworth sought to place an emphasis on the recovery of feeling, imagination, spontaneity and the 'authentic' self, and his commitment to investing poetry with 'incidents and situations from common life' and to employing wherever possible 'a selection of the language really spoken by men'[9] meant that his writings had a democratic edge to them which can be seen as part of that wider concern with egalitarianism prevalent in the Romantic period.

EBB's admiration for Wordsworth began early and she remained dedicated to him throughout her career in a manner which was comparable with the hero-worship she so often explores in her political writings. In her review of his *Poems, Chiefly of Early and Late Years*, included in her essay on British poetry published in the *Athenaeum* in 1842, for example, she emphasizes Wordsworth's position as the 'poet-hero of a movement essential to the better being of poetry' and as the 'poet-prophet of utterances greater than those who first listened could comprehend, and ... influences most vital and expansive' (*Works* 4:510). As with Beattie's Edwin, then, Wordsworth is established here as a prophetic figure, that model of poet which, as J. R. Watson notes, recalls traditional concepts of the bard and is often linked to notions of national consciousness.[10] Indeed, it was this view of Wordsworth as bard-like visionary which EBB explicitly advanced in her sonnet 'On a Portrait of Wordsworth by B. R. Haydon', written in 1842 and included in *Poems* (1844):

> Wordsworth upon Helvellyn! Let the cloud
> Ebb audibly along the mountain-wind
> Then break against the rock, and show behind
> The lowland valleys floating up to crowd
> The sense with beauty. He with forehead bowed
> And humble-lidded eyes, as one inclined
> Before the sovran thought of his own mind,
> And very meek with inspirations proud,
> Takes here his rightful place as poet-priest
> By the high altar, singing prayer and prayer
> To the higher Heavens. A noble vision free
> Our Haydon's hand has flung out from the mist!
> No portrait this, with Academic air!
> This is the poet and his poetry.

EBB's youngest sister, Arabella, had seen this portrait, now housed in London's National Portrait Gallery, in Haydon's studio and had arranged for it to be sent to Wimpole Street for EBB to view. EBB subsequently used the painting as the basis of one of her key ekphrasis poems (poems that take a work of art as their subject) in which she explores what Wordsworth means to her both in terms of his status and the nature of his poetry.

Interestingly, the sonnet reverses our viewing experience of the portrait itself where the eye is immediately struck by the figure of Wordsworth dominating the canvas before moving out to observe the surrounding natural scenery. EBB's sonnet rather describes the backdrop of clouds and rocks first and then focuses in on the poet, a technique which significantly withholds the depiction of the subject until the fifth line. The poem emphasizes, as does the painting itself, the poet with 'forehead bowed', deep in 'sovran thought' and almost overpowered by his own imagination, before which he is humble and 'meek'. And yet, in a neat shift at the sonnet's volta, EBB argues that it is precisely this humble posture which enables Wordsworth to take 'his rightful place as poet-priest' and his writings, as a version of prayer, to connect spiritually '[t]o the higher Heavens'.

For EBB, then, Wordsworth represented the great prophetic poet, the man at one with nature whose imagination was able to yield access to spiritual truths. Certainly, Wordsworth's influence on her own work can be felt throughout poems as varied as 'Memory' (1826), 'A Sea-Side Walk' (1838), 'Man and Nature' (1838) and, with its emphasis on nature as moral guide, 'Lessons from the Gorse' (1844):

> Mountain gorses, do ye teach us
> From that academic chair,
> Canopied with azure air,
> That the wisest word man reaches
> Is the humblest he can speak?
> Ye, who live on mountain peak,
> Yet live low along the ground, beside the grasses meek!
>
> (ll.15–21)

It is little wonder then, that when EBB met Wordsworth at John Kenyon's house in 1836, she came away rhapsodizing: 'I never walked in the skies before; & perhaps never shall again, when so many stars are out' (*Correspondence* 3:217).

Of the Romantics, however, it is arguably George Gordon, Lord Byron (1788-1824) who had the greatest impact on EBB in the initial years of her development and whose approach to the relations between poetry and the wider world would resonate throughout her career from her early publications to those final works published posthumously in *Last Poems* (1862). EBB was drawn to Byron's poetry from an early age – she wrote to her Uncle Samuel in 1818, for example, that the fourth canto of *Childe Harold* contains descriptions in which '[a]ll the energy, all the sublimity of modern verse is centered' (*Correspondence* 1:67) – and she certainly appears to have viewed Byron as the embodiment of that active poet with whom she wanted to align herself. Indeed, as EBB later admitted to Mary Russell Mitford, as a young girl she had 'a determinate resolution to dress up in men's clothes as soon as ever I was free of the nursery, & go into the world "to seek my fortune". "*How*", was not decided; but I rather leant towards being Lord Byron's PAGE' (*Mitford* 2:7).

Significantly, it was Byron's commitment to politics which particularly attracted EBB and especially his involvement in the Greek War of Independence. Greece had been under Turkish rule since the fifteenth century but from the mid-eighteenth century onwards, and particularly following the outbreak of the French Revolution and the spread of nationalist ideas, many Greeks sought to reclaim control over their country and bring about national self-agency. There was tremendous support for Greek independence across Europe amongst those intellectuals whose classical studies had led them to view Greece as one of the major origins of Western civilization, yet Byron was famous not only for his intellectual and literary support of the Greek cause, but for actually going out to the country in 1823 to fight in the struggle. Within four months of his arrival at Missolonghi, however, the village where he had landed in full martial uniform complete with Homeric helmet, he was dead, probably from Mediterranean tick-fever. As Jennifer Wallace notes, this event had massive symbolic importance in the history of the Greek struggle,[11] and EBB subsequently used it as the basis for one of her first public works, 'Stanzas on the Death of Lord Byron'. Initially published in the *Globe and Traveller* and then reprinted in *An Essay on Mind, and Other Poems*, this is one of EBB's most interesting elegies as she focuses on the multiple losses embodied in Byron's death:

> He *was*, and *is* not! Græcia's trembling shore,
> Sighing through all her palmy groves, shall tell
> That Harold's pilgrimage at last is o'er –
> Mute the impassioned tongue, and tuneful shell,
> That erst was wont in noblest strains to swell –

Hush'd the proud shouts that rode Ægæa's wave!
For lo! the great Deliv'rer breathes farewell!
Gives to the world his mem'ry and a grave –
Expiring in the land he only lived to save!

>   .   .   .   .   .   .

Britannia's Poet! Græcia's hero, sleeps!
And Freedom, bending o'er the breathless clay,
Lifts up her voice, and in her anguish weeps!
For *us*, a night hath clouded o'er our day,
And hush'd the lips that breath'd our fairest lay.
Alas! and must the British lyre resound
A requiem, while the spirit wings away
Of him who on its strings such music found,
And taught its startling chords to give so sweet a sound!

>   (ll.1–9; 19–27)

As he is constructed here, Byron is a mythologized figure, aligned with his own Childe Harold as both 'Britannia's Poet' and 'Græcia's hero' and represented as the 'great Deliv'rer' whose death is lamented by 'the land he only lived to save'. And yet whilst the great singer/poet is now physically silenced, EBB suggests in the poem's last stanza that his 'music' will live on in his 'grave...thick with voices' (l.34). The grave therefore becomes ambiguously associated with both bodily decay and the possibility of everlasting presence, an idea which EBB would utilize again two decades later in her fable-poem, 'The Poet and the Bird' (1844).[12]

Byron thus represents the archetypal poet-politician for EBB and it is this belief that poetry has crucial political work to do which she embraces from an early stage. Indeed, as I discuss in more detail in Chapter 4, EBB was actively involved in political debate from a young age, encouraged in particular by the alignment of the Barrett family men with the Whigs, the party which had at its core that commitment to the dignity and freedom of the individual which underlies much of EBB's poetry. But is also seems reasonable to argue that EBB's sustained commitment to politics was derived, at least in part, from her understanding that many of her great poetic predecessors and contemporaries, including Wordsworth, Byron and Shelley, were themselves politically driven and used their writings to expose oppression of all kinds and, often, to envisage a more optimistic political future. Indeed, EBB would no doubt have held with

Shelley's famous assertion in *A Defence of Poetry* that poets are the 'unacknowledged legislators of the World.'[13]

This commitment to the political work of poetry runs throughout EBB's writings from the outset. Her first major work, for example, is the four-book epic, *The Battle of Marathon*, written during 1817–19 and privately printed by her father in 1820 for her fourteenth birthday. It is an astonishing start for the poet in many respects – in its length (over 1400 lines), its complex engagement with epic conventions, and its choice of subject: the defeat of the invading Persian army by the vastly outnumbered Athenian troops on the plains of Marathon in 490BC, an event which is often viewed as pivotal to the process of Greece's developing democracy. As I have suggested elsewhere, in the context of early nineteenth-century philhellenism and the push to free modern Greece from Turkish occupation, this focus is highly pertinent.[14] Moreover, the poem is accompanied by a lucid and surprisingly uninhibited preface in which EBB lays bare her views on the centrality of poetry to social and political development. For as she forcefully claims, poetry is '[t]he noblest of the productions of man' which 'elevates the mind to Heaven' (*Works* 4:15) and which, through the writings of Homer, was key to the emergence of the ancient Greeks from a benighted society into a fledgling civilization:

> Then it was that Greece began to give those immortal examples of exalted feeling, and of patriotic virtue, which have since astonished the world; then it was that the unenlightened soul of the savage rose above the degradation which assimilated him to the brute creation, and discovered the first rays of social independence, and of limited freedom; not the freedom of barbarism, but that of a state enlightened by a wise jurisdiction, and restrained by civil laws. (*Works* 4:16)

There are few passages in EBB's work before *Aurora Leigh* that make so powerful a case for her belief in poetry as a civilizing political force. And as if EBB needed to hammer home her conviction further, she opens the final paragraph of the preface with the assertion that 'Poetry is the parent of liberty' (*Works* 4:19). Clearly, then, *The Battle of Marathon* is evidence of EBB's starting to shape her poetics in such a way as to situate the poet at the centre of society, culture and politics, rather than marginal to them, with the assurance that poetry has the potential to engender debate, galvanize change and transform opinion –

11

that model of poet promoted by the major Romantics and which Thomas Carlyle (1795–1881), the key Victorian sage and EBB's friend in the 1840s and 1850s, would term the *vates* figure.[15] In adopting this model, of course, EBB was clearly rejecting dominant ideas concerning the middle-class woman's allotted sphere and aligning herself with what was fundamentally a male construction, originally associated with Old Testament prophets. And yet, although the notion of the *vates* figure offers a general trajectory for reading EBB's poetics, this is not to suggest that her views on poetry and what poetry could achieve were static or unshifting, nor that the *vates* model was unqualified or unquestioned by her. Indeed, given the length of her career, this is unsurprising. Rather, it is possible to view EBB's poetic development in terms of a series of key shifts which can be mapped, in broad terms at least, onto the different decades through which she lived and wrote.

Following *The Battle of Marathon*, EBB continued her political concerns with liberty and the Greek question in her first properly published verses, the three lyric poems 'Stanzas, excited by some reflections on the present state of Greece' (*New Monthly Magazine*, May 1821), 'Thoughts awakened by contemplating a piece of the palm which grows on the summit of the Athenian Acropolis' (*New Monthly Magazine*, July 1821), and the poem I have already discussed, 'Stanzas on the Death of Lord Byron'. Although published under her initials rather than her full name, these poems show EBB's entry into the public sphere as a political rather than a confessional poet, addressing contemporary issues rather than generalized sentiment, and employing often powerful rhetoric rather than solely the language of the emotions. These initial works were then followed by her major volume of the decade, *An Essay on Mind, and Other Poems*, the title work of which, as I noted above, expressly links poetry with expansive thinking and intellectual liberty. The final part of the poem, however, extends this argument to suggest that those figures who are most intellec-tually liberated – such as EBB's hero Byron, whom she terms 'the Mont Blanc of intellect' (l.70) – have the ability to engender the physical liberation of countries like Greece from the fetters of political occupation and oppression. Greece is explicitly celebrated in Book Two of the poem as the 'country of my soul' (l.1147), and in the preface to the poem, which echoes the preface to *The Battle of Marathon*, EBB again stresses that poetry is linked to the possibilities of nationalism. For 'while we behold in poetry, the inspiritings to political feeling, the "monumentum ære perennius" [monument more durable than bronze[16]] of buried nations, we are loth to believe her unequal to the higher walks of intellect' (*Works* 4:78). At this stage of her career, then, it seems likely that EBB would have echoed Byron's sentiments when he commented that 'If I am a poet... the air of Greece has made me one.'[17]

It is important to draw attention here to another key concern of the preface: EBB's forceful rejection of the idea that 'poetry is not a proper vehicle for abstract ideas'. For as she argues, 'We do not deem the imaginative incompatible with the philosophic, for the name of Bacon is on our lips; then why should we expel the argumentative from the limits of the poetic?' (*Works* 4:77). This belief in poetry as a medium for argument and debate is one which EBB would hold to throughout her career as part of her conviction that poetry is more intellectually engaged than the novel or even non-fictional prose. And yet the youthful confidence which EBB expresses in *An Essay on Mind* and its preface does not remain untempered across the volume as a whole. For in the final poem of the collection, 'The Vision of Fame', EBB depicts an encounter between the speaker and a beautiful, *femme-fatale*-like figure who sings of the possibility of achieving immortality through song/poetry. Indeed, in keeping with the overall agenda of *An Essay on Mind*, the vision even suggests that poets might be able to use their work politically so that 'Nations may rise' (l.70). But as the speaker becomes increasingly attracted to this figure, her flesh suddenly starts to curl up from her bones, '[l]ike to a blasted scroll' (l.84) – a possible image of the danger associated with the written word – and drops away to leave 'a bleachëd skeleton/ Where erst was ladye bright!' (ll.87–8). This gothic metamorphosis, where all bodily boundaries dissolve and only the 'vacant sockets' of the eyes are left gleaming (l.89), thus provides a terrifying conclusion to a volume which repeatedly foregrounds the fame of heroic men. For here the practice of art solely for prestige and renown is exposed as being ultimately illusory and self-destructive: 'Woe's me,' concludes the speaker, 'for THIS is

FAME' (1.96). EBB would always be fascinated by fame and particularly the nature of literary celebrity – she herself, of course, would rapidly rise to national and international status over the next couple of decades and she and Robert would be viewed by many as Florence's celebrity couple when they settled there in the late 1840s[18] – yet the anxieties raised in 'The Vision of Fame' regarding ambition, status, and the nature of artistic production were ones which would keep resurfacing to a greater or lesser degree throughout her lifetime.

As EBB's career entered the 1830s, a letter to Hugh Stuart Boyd concerning French poetry offers some clues to her developing sense of her own poetics. As she writes:

> The French have no part or lot in poetry. I am more & more convinced that they have *none*. A gentleman in this neighbourhood has been justly criticised for having the borders of a pond near his house levelled & rolled, by which he of course destroyed every picturesque roughness & undulation. The French do just the same with the banks of their Helicon. They are all made smooth & neat & clean & uninteresting. Every neighbouring spot is worked into a parterre. Even sublime & terrible subjects are cultivated with much the same attention to preciseness – laid out, like the burial ground near Paris, with trim shrubs, mown grass, & gravel walks! – (*Correspondence* 2:253)

This is a telling criticism which prefigures Charlotte Brontë's similarly phrased comments on Jane Austen's fiction being like 'a carefully-fenced, highly cultivated garden, with neat borders and delicate flowers – but no glance of a bright vivid physiognomy – no open country – no fresh air – no blue hill – no bonny beck.'[19] Both EBB and Brontë set out their stall against such overly-'cultivated' literary writing, seeking instead to take risks and leave the raw edges unpolished. And it was often this unwillingness to make things 'smooth & neat & clean' for which both writers were condemned by reviewers. In EBB's case, her use of compound words, archaisms, internal rhymes and near rhymes was frequently criticized in reviews (the rhyming of 'panther' with 'saunter' and 'angels' with 'candles' in 'The Dead Pan' was objected to, for example)[20] and she was repeatedly maligned for what the *North American Review* termed her 'lawless extravagance' (*Correspondence* 6:376). Such condemnation had little impact on EBB, however, who continued to experiment with language, form and subject matter throughout her career, pushing at the boundaries of expectations surrounding nineteenth-century poetry and consequently shaping an often highly-original poetics.

During the 1830s, EBB's work underwent a significant shift as that overt engagement with politics which characterizes much of her poetry in the 1820s seems to fade into the background and her poems become dominated by larger mythic subjects and a concern with religious issues and debates. As I have argued previously, however, it is wrong to assume that EBB became 'de-politicized' at this point since her diary and correspondence reveal an ongoing interest in issues as varied as the 1830 July Revolution in France, the passing of the First Reform Bill in Britain, and the implications of Victoria's accession to the throne. In her poetry, too, the concerns with power and oppression which are central to her political thought are still present although they are often dealt with more obliquely.[21] Her 1833 collection, *Prometheus Bound, and Miscellaneous Poems*, for example, is structured around her own translation of Æschylus' classical tragedy, a work which had been such a central source of inspiration for the previous generation of artists (including Byron, Shelley and Beethoven) and which can be seen, as Linda M. Lewis notes, as the 'Ur-myth of the romantic age'.[22] The narrative of the archetypal rebel figure, who steals fire from the gods in order to give it to humankind and who is then punished by Zeus by being chained to a rock and having his regenerative liver torn out daily by an eagle, deals with key political issues which fascinated EBB such as the nature of tyranny, structures of authoritarianism, and physical and psychological violence. Further, the play importantly speaks of the possibilities of resistance in Prometheus' refusing to give Zeus the name of his future usurper, thereby articulating, in James Scully's phrasing, 'a war between brute force and unbending knowledge'.[23] Although EBB would later criticize the quality of her translation, calling it 'stiff & hard – a Prometheus *twice* bound' (*Correspondence* 5:26), the issues raised in the play would nevertheless remain central to her poetics overall. Certainly, the ongoing relevance of the text for her thinking is evident in her re-translating it in the 1840s, a decade of major social and political upheaval in both Britain and Europe, and including it in *Poems* (1850).

15

Five years after the *Prometheus* volume, EBB published her most important collection to date, *The Seraphim, and Other Poems* (1838), which was also the first volume to appear under her full name (the previous volumes had been published either anonymously or under her initials). The collection marks an important new phase of experimentation, which is witnessed in particular in the title poem, the subject of which came to mind, EBB notes in the preface, whilst she was translating *Prometheus Bound*. I discuss *The Seraphim* in detail in Chapter 2, but it is important to highlight here how the poem, which centres on two angels debating key religious issues while they watch the Crucifixion from heaven, is one of EBB's most important works of the 1830s and, like many of her lyric poems of the period, far more complex in terms of the politics of religion than is often acknowledged. Moreover, as Karen Dieleman has persuasively argued, *The Seraphim*, along with 'The Virgin Mary to the Child Jesus' (1838) and the later *A Drama of Exile* (1844), shows EBB engaging with a different model of poet to the *vates*, that of the preacher, which Dieleman links specifically to EBB's commitment to Congregationalism (see Chapter 2).[24] Certainly, *The Seraphim* is an extremely innovative opening to a collection which also sees EBB starting to experiment with the ballad form in 'A Romance of the Ganges' and conventions of nature poetry in works such as 'The Deserted Garden' and 'An Island'.

In the preface to the *Seraphim* volume, EBB makes an explicit connection between the poet and religion which is highly significant for an understanding of her poetics in this decade and beyond:

> 'An irreligious poet,' said Burns, meaning an undevotional one, 'is a monster.' An irreligious poet, he might have said, is no poet at all. The gravitation of poetry is upwards. The poetic wing, if it move, ascends. (*Works* 4:292)

This sense of the devotional poet is borne out in the volume not only in the title work, but also in the elegaic 'Cowper's Grave', written to celebrate the eighteenth-century poet, classicist and hymn writer, William Cowper (1731–1800). As with 'Stanzas on the Death of Lord Byron', EBB's poem to Cowper centres on his final resting place as a means of contemplating both his importance as a writer and the nature and role of poetry itself.

For despite Cowper's 'shattered brain' (l.21), as EBB terms it (he was plagued by severe depression throughout his life), and despite his increasing blindness, Cowper is constructed in the poem as a model of what a writer could hope to be:

He shall be strong to sanctify the poet's high vocation,
And bow the meekest Christian down in meeker adoration.
Nor ever shall he be, in praise, by wise or good forsaken,
Named softly as the household name of one whom God hath taken.

(ll.13–16)

In suffering for his art and maintaining his devotion to God, the poem suggests, Cowper will achieve both spiritual redemption in Heaven and literary fame beyond his death. Significantly, this notion of the artist would also form the basis of the long work 'A Vision of Poets', included in *Poems* (1844), where, EBB writes in the preface, she 'endeavoured to indicate the necessary relations of genius to suffering and self-sacrifice' and to emphasize 'the mission of the poet, of the self-abnegation implied in it, of the great work involved in it' (*Works* 2:569). Suffering, sacrifice, hard work: these elements, along with a commitment to religion, remain at the core of EBB's conception of the poet through to *Aurora Leigh* and beyond.

The other poem in the *Seraphim* volume that deals explicitly with the figure of the poet is 'The Poet's Vow', a five-part work which explores the decision of the eponymous poet (he remains significantly unnamed throughout) to break with all human relations and remove to an isolated mansion in 'a stagnant place apart' (l.54). Disengaged from the social world, he purposely ignores the representatives of religion (three Christians), love (a married couple), and hope for the future (a playing child) who pass by his window, in a manner which constitutes, EBB emphasizes, both an affront to nature and an affront to God. Indeed, the poem is clear about the effects of this '[r]ejection of ... humanness' (l.266) since the poet is plunged into a state of terrifying introspection from which he is shaken only by the arrival of the dead body of his previous betrothed, Rosalind. Through the words written on a scroll attached to her corpse, Rosalind is then able to rebuke the poet posthumously for his desertion of her and to warn of even more dire consequences:

17

'I charge thee, by the living's prayer,
    And the dead's silentness,
To wring from out thy soul a cry
    Which God shall hear and bless!
Lest Heaven's own palm droop in my hand,
And pale among the saints I stand,
    A saint companionless.'

(ll.450–6)

As Helen Cooper notes, it takes the woman's message to challenge 'the sterility of [the poet's] aesthetic', with the result that he dies from the grief accompanying his realization.[25] As with Beattie's *The Minstrel*, then, or Tennyson's 'The Palace of Art' (1832), 'The Poet's Vow' provides a warning against embracing artistic solipsism to the extent that it becomes, quite literally, deadly. For as EBB highlights in the preface, 'the creature cannot be *isolated* from the creature' (*Works* 4:291) and the poet who seeks to galvanize change cannot be isolated from humanity and the social world.

By this stage in her career, EBB's own relations with the social world had altered considerably for she was now living in London, enabling her to make connections with key literary figures (her friendships with her cousin John Kenyon and the novelist Mary Russell Mitford would be particularly important to her career) and placing her at the heart of the British political scene. Indeed, despite her increasing inability to leave her room because of her illness – she wrote to Mitford of 'this shutting up...which is necessary to prevent the tendency to organic disease of the lungs' (*Mitford* 3:142) – she nevertheless maintained a keen interest in contemporary affairs through reading and her epistolary relationships. Consequently, when her new collection, *Poems*, appeared in 1844, it evidenced her revitalized and explicit engagement with politics and social issues throughout. In 'The Cry of the Children', for example, EBB exposes the horrors of child employment which she had read about in parliamentary reports, while 'The Cry of the Human' interrogates the problems associated with the Corn Laws, agricultural workers and *laissez-faire* capitalism. Poems such as 'The Romaunt of the Page' and 'The Romance of the Swan's Nest' explore the power structures of relationships in various social environments and under various social pressures.

'Crowned and Wedded' and 'Crowned and Buried' examine the possibilities and limitations of the different leadership styles of Queen Victoria and Napoleon Bonaparte respectively. And the highly impressive and intriguing 'Lady Geraldine's Courtship', the poem that triggered thoughts of the modern epic that would become *Aurora Leigh*, consolidated EBB's concern with the contemporary in its very subtitle, 'A Romance of the Age'. (I discuss these poems in more detail in Chapters 3 and 4.) Before *Aurora Leigh*, *Poems* was EBB's most critically acclaimed work and saw her firmly adopting that position of commentator on socio-political concerns which she would maintain for the rest of her career. And yet despite this resurgence of confidence, or maybe because of it, *Poems* also sees EBB attempting to work through and put to rest a set of specific anxieties about gender and her position in relation to other *women* poets which had been worrying her for nearly a decade.

In particular, these anxieties were bound up with EBB's perception of her key contemporaries, Felicia Hemans (1793–1835), the writer of poems such as 'Casabianca' and 'Homes of England', and L.E.L. (Laetitia Elizabeth Landon, 1802–38), whose works include *The Improvisatrice* and 'A History of the Lyre'. Both poets were extremely prolific and highly popular and yet whilst recent work by critics such as Tricia Lootens and Emma Mason has started to reread their work as potentially subversive,[26] EBB found their seeming emphasis on the affections, conventional piety and patriotic rhetoric both limited and constraining. In her elegy for Hemans, for example, which was included in the *Seraphim* volume, EBB is clearly ambivalent about Hemans' achievements, noting that while the 'bay-crowned' poet 'drew from rocky earth and man, abstractions high and moving' (ll.1; 23), she was nevertheless only able to produce a 'silver song' (significantly not gold) since 'her part in life was mourning' (ll.31; 17). This public damning with faint praise gives way to more explicit criticism in the correspondence with Mary Russell Mitford, where, despite acknowledging Hemans' 'high moral tone', EBB condemns her 'smoothness', her seeming monotony, and that 'refinement' which 'like the prisoner's iron...enters into her soul' (*Mitford* 2:88). Similarly, in the elegy which she wrote for Landon, 'LEL's Last Question' (included in *Poems*, 1844), EBB emphasizes LEL's disabling need for popularity ('Do you think of me as I think of you?' is the repeated refrain) and her severely limited subject matter:

> Love-learnéd she had sung of love and love, –
> And like a child that, sleeping with dropt head
> Upon the fairy-book he lately read,
> Whatever household noises round him move,
> Hears in his dream some elfin turbulence, –
> Even so, suggestive to her inward sense,
> All sounds of life assumed one tune of love.
>
> (ll.15–21)

LEL is constructed here as naïve and inexperienced, inhabiting an unreal 'fairy' world rather than the 'real' socio-political world into which EBB increasingly inserts herself and her writings. Indeed, the fact that this stanza opens and closes with the word 'love' confirms the suffocating constrictions which EBB associates with LEL's work. Further, in the more overtly critical comments in the correspondence with Mitford, EBB suggests that LEL's writing lacks an informed, intellectual basis since 'the strength of our *feelings*, often rises up out of our *thoughts*' and '[h]er genius was not strong enough to assert itself in truth' (*Correspondence* 3:194; 5:72).

As Anne K. Mellor notes, both Hemans and LEL 'self-consciously embraced an aesthetic of the beautiful' and subscribed to 'a specifically "feminine" poetry'.[27] It was this conservative 'feminine' poetry of the affections which EBB consistently defined herself against, seeking instead to engage with a more overtly socio-political and 'masculine' poetics associated with the male Romantics and, before them, Dante and Milton – even if, as I explore in the following chapters, she often subtly modified this poetics in order to assert her own voice and perspective. Indeed, her perception of the limitations of women poets might be one reason why, apart from Sappho, the supposed founder of lyric poetry, women are absent from the vast transnational procession of ancient and modern poets in 'A Vision of Poets' and why, in 1845, EBB famously lamented the lack of 'poetic grandmothers' in the British literary tradition (*Correspondence* 10:14).

Significantly, the one contemporary woman artist who *is* celebrated in *Poems* (1844) is George Sand (1804–76), the controversial French novelist, cross-dresser, socialist and proto-feminist who EBB makes the focus of two of her most important and frequently-anthologized sonnets: 'To George Sand: A Desire' and 'To George Sand: A Recognition'. Heralded as 'Thou large-brained woman and large-hearted man' ('A Desire', l.1) and 'True genius, but true woman!' ('A Recognition', l.1), Sand is seen to embody an almost dual-gendered/androgynous subject position which EBB views as particularly productive for the creation of art in the modern world.[28] But although Sand is clearly influential on the construction of Aurora Leigh (as many commentators have noted, Aurora's name recalls Sand's real name, Amandine Aurore Lucile Dupin) and although EBB wrote that 'if she is not the first female genius of any country or age I really do not know who is' (Correspondence 10:15), Sand is still principally a novelist, not a poet. Once again, therefore, EBB is forced to forge her own path as a new kind of (woman) poet, seeking a new voice for the modern age.

Within three years, however, EBB's life and career were utterly transformed when, following the publication of Poems with its explicit celebration of Robert Browning's work in 'Lady Geraldine's Courtship', EBB was contacted by the younger poet and twenty months later they secretly married. Mary Sanders Pollock has carefully detailed the phenomenal 'Creative Partner-ship' which developed between the two poets,[29] one early outcome of which was the astonishing Sonnets from the Portuguese (published in the revised and expanded edition of Poems, 1850). A sequence of forty-four interconnected Petrarchan sonnets which, on one level at least, records the complexities of EBB's developing love for Robert, Sonnets from the Portuguese effectively rewrote the map of sonnet composition in the nineteenth century, subverting and reconfiguring established models (in particular, enabling the woman to speak rather than remaining the silenced object of address) and having a huge influence on later sonneteers such as Christina Rossetti, Dante Gabriel Rossetti and Augusta Webster. Indeed, the sonnets are now being reread as far more challenging and complex than has often been acknowledged, as witnessed even in what is arguably EBB's most famous and popular poem, Sonnet 43:

> How do I love thee? Let me count the ways.
> I love thee to the depth and breadth and height

My soul can reach, when feeling out of sight
For the ends of Being and ideal Grace.
I love thee to the level of everyday's
Most quiet need, by sun and candlelight.
I love thee freely, as men strive for Right;
I love thee purely, as they turn from Praise.
I love thee with the passion put to use
In my old griefs, and with my childhood's faith.
I love thee with a love I seemed to lose
With my lost saints, – I love thee with the breath,
Smiles, tears, of all my life! – and, if God choose,
I shall but love thee better after death.

With its repeated syntactical structure of 'I love thee', employed nine times in fourteen lines, this poem articulates the all-encompassing nature of the speaker's emotion which seemingly transcends time and space and is near impossible to define. Indeed, what the repetitions here signify is the speaker's inability to find a fully adequate expression of how she loves, as she shifts from metaphysical comparisons in the opening lines through to associations with first the 'everyday' and then the political ('I love thee freely, as men strive for Right'). More radically, the poem proceeds to suggest that the emotion felt for the beloved replaces the speaker's religion, her 'childhood's faith' and 'lost saints'. For whilst the speaker returns to God in the penultimate line, the final emphasis is on an afterlife with the beloved which might simultaneously suggest a qualification of established religion: heaven will not be enough without her beloved there. As I note further in Chapter 3, *Sonnets from the Portuguese* challenges all kinds of conventions and belief systems, and certainly the sequence served to confirm once again EBB's position as one of the most ground-breaking poets of the age.

Following their marriage in September 1846, the Brownings emigrated to Italy where, except for short periods in France, they were to remain until EBB's death in 1861. This relocation to the land associated with many of those Romantic poets who had been such an influence on both EBB and Robert in earlier years also placed them at the centre of an established Anglo-American literary community in Florence which included other committed, if not so skilled, women poets such as Eliza Ogilvy

(1822–1912), Isa Blagden (1817?–73) and Theodosia Garrow Trollope (1825–65). As Alison Chapman has shown in her insightful work on this community, 'the identity of the woman expatriate poet, displaced from her own nation and audience' was 'often creatively and professionally enabling'.[30] Certainly the physical and psychological distance from England allowed EBB to develop her poetics in innovative ways and to tackle both more experimental forms and more challenging subjects. This comes through, for example, in the powerful poem, 'The Runaway Slave at Pilgrim's Point', which, although begun in London, was the first poem EBB completed in her newly-adopted homeland. With its forthright representation of the horrors of American slavery told through the voice of a raped black female slave who subsequently commits infanticide as a symbolic attack on the 'master-right' (l.126), this is EBB's most compelling use of the dramatic monologue, that major development in nineteenth-century poetry which would become most associated with her husband Robert in subsequent decades (see Chapter 4).

It was, however, Italy itself and the political struggle for Italian unification and freedom from Austrian control (the *Risorgimento*) which was to dominate EBB's poetics for the rest of her career in one form or another. This concern first manifests itself in the challenging *Casa Guidi Windows* (1851), EBB's most overtly political poem to date and the poem where she most clearly employs the Carlylean vatic voice. A two-part work which was written over the politically-volatile period of 1847–51, it records in Part 1 the hopes for a liberated Italy galvanized by Grand Duke Leopold's concessions to the Tuscan people, and, in Part 2, the despair when those hopes were lost following the defeat of the revolutions of 1848–9. Structurally, the piece is particularly intriguing, centring on two processions – that of the people celebrating in carnival style, and that of the Austrian soldiers marching through the city to restore reactionary control over the state – which take place outside EBB's apartment on Casa Guidi. As critics such as Julia Markus and Isobel Armstrong have argued, the windows of the title therefore function both to frame the political events occurring outside and to establish the speaker as observer and commentator.[31] Certainly, the resulting work is strong and forthright as EBB critiques military leadership in the figure of Leopold (an 'illegitimate Caesar', Part 2, l.86), established religion in the figure of Pope Pius IX (who 'prefer[s]/ "The interests of the Church"' to liberal reform, 1:999–1000), and the Italian people themselves for their general lack of direction and organisation, having 'no knowledge, no conception, nought' (2:202).

Yet as EBB asserts in the opening verse paragraphs, a new kind of poetics is needed if this subject is to be treated effectively. For most poets and singers who have lamented Italy's oppression by the Austrians have tended to rely upon stereotypical images of the country as an injured or deserted woman – 'shamed sister' or 'Juliet of nations' (1:25; 36) – and have used extensive metaphor and beautiful language to the degree that the political message is buried ('sheathed in music', 1:18) and consequently ineffectual. As EBB criticizes, "tis easier to gaze long/ On mournful masks, and sad effigies/ Than on real, live, weak creatures crushed by strong' (1:46–8). What is required, therefore, is a new work which will bring energy back to the political drive for unification. Taking her inspiration not from inherited traditions but from a boy singing 'O bella libertà, O bella!' (1:3) beneath her apartment window – a key symbol of hope for the future since 'the heart of Italy must beat,/ While such a voice ha[s] leave to rise serene' (1:8–9) – EBB asserts that her own poem will be just such a new song, thereby enabling her to speak for those 'who stand in Italy to-day' (1:49).

This commitment to the cause of the *Risorgimento* would remain central to EBB's poetics for the rest of her career. Indeed, she would return overtly to writing about Italian politics in the final collection she saw to press before her death, *Poems Before Congress* (1860), a slim volume of eight poems which includes some of her most controversial and compelling works and which critics such as Elizabeth Woodworth and Katherine Montwieler are beginning to reveal as highly complex and important.[32] Moreover, EBB continued to focus on the problems of unification in some of those works written just before her death, including the fascinating 'Mother and Poet' which sees her still trying to work through the relations between poetry, gender and politics that have informed her poetics for decades (see Conclusion).

And then, of course, in the middle of *Casa Guidi Windows* and *Poems Before Congress* is the poem for which EBB is rightly most famous, *Aurora Leigh* (1856), that 'most mature of my works' as EBB terms it in the Dedication. As I explore in detail in Chapter 5, the innovations in form, subject matter, language and style in this poem are intricate and multilayered as EBB interrogates the professional development of a woman poet in the modern world. By transforming the classical epic that she had been drawn to in her youthful *Battle of Marathon* into a new nine-book, gynocentric epic, and by incorporating the conversational style and contemporary subject matters of nineteenth-century social-realist fiction, EBB developed her most generically-complex work, the 'novel-in-verse', which she saw as the most suitable form for dealing with what Aurora terms 'this live, throbbing age' (5:203). Indeed, right at the very heart of this poem, in Book 5, is possibly Victorian literature's most compelling articulation of the need to write a new modern poetics and not to be caught unproductively in the past:

> ...if there's room for poets in this world
> A little overgrown, (I think there is)
> Their sole work is to represent the age,
> Their age, not Charlemagne's,—this live, throbbing age,
> That brawls, cheats, maddens, calculates, aspires,
> And spends more passion, more heroic heat,
> Betwixt the mirrors of its drawing-rooms,
> Than Roland with his knights at Roncesvalles.
>
> .   .   .   .   .   .
>   Never flinch,
> But still, unscrupulously epic, catch
> Upon the burning lava of a song
> The full-veined, heaving, double-breasted Age:
> That, when the next shall come, the men of that
> May touch the impress with reverent hand, and say
> 'Behold, – behold the paps we all have sucked!
> This bosom seems to beat still, or at least
> It sets ours beating: this is living art,
> Which thus presents and thus records true life.'
>
> (5:200–7; 213–22)

'Never flinch,' asserts Aurora, in one of EBB's key manifestos, but write 'unscrupulously' of the modern age, thereby creating 'the burning lava of a song.' It is a powerful clarion call from a writer who, throughout her career, constantly wrote about poetry in a self-reflexive manner, examining and rethinking the role of the poet and exploring the function of poetry in the social world. Few poets seem to have constantly interrogated their own vocation so overtly, so publicly and so obsessively, pointing to a very real need on EBB's part to develop a secure position in relation to inherited traditions and to forge a new poetics which was both meaningful and relevant. It was a hard-fought battle, but one which finally saw EBB asserting her right to be a prophetic spokeswoman of her age. For it was in the midst of socio-political controversy and debate that EBB eventually found a home as the creator of that 'living art' which transformed her into one of the most important and challenging poets of the nineteenth century. As I start to explore in the next chapter, however, the envisioning of a home for the speakers and protagonists of her own poems was often far more fraught.

2

The Search for a Spiritual Home

In the last chapter I explored some of the ways in which EBB shaped and reconfigured her poetics across the course of her career, demonstrating how she engaged with and revised inherited traditions in order to establish herself as a major poet who examines, questions and critiques her 'live, throbbing age' (*Aurora Leigh*, 5:203). The 'home' which she found for herself as a poet was carefully and precisely fashioned and it subsequently enabled her to master a wide range of forms and styles and to speak out on a wide range of social and political concerns. As with Aurora Leigh, EBB viewed poetry as her true vocation from the outset and would always confidently assert, 'I too have... work to do' (2:455).

In this chapter, I start to consider the ways in which the speakers and protagonists of EBB's poems are also often depicted in the search for a 'home', the nature of which, as I suggested in the preface, is shifting and fluid and defined in multiple ways. I pay particular attention here to four poems that EBB wrote across the 1830s and 1840s – two of them the lead poems of key volumes – which explore what I have termed in the chapter title the search for a spiritual home. Religion was always important to EBB's poetics and yet this is an area which has only recently received serious critical attention. In her 1989 study, *Elizabeth Barrett Browning: Origins of a New Poetry*, for example, Dorothy Mermin suggested that EBB's religious poems are somewhat simplistic and naïve in their treatment of spiritual issues, and certainly far more so than the works of other religious poets of the period such as Christina Rossetti and Gerard Manley Hopkins.[1] This reading may partly arise because, as Julia Neuberger notes in the introduction to her anthology of women's spiritual poetry, *The Things That Matter* (1992), feminist critics have often tended to react against the seemingly 'private, unassertive nature' of religious writing.[2] Over the last ten years or so, however, EBB's religious poetry has started to be reassessed through the work of critics such as Linda M. Lewis and Karen Dieleman, work which reveals EBB's theological and spiritual engagement to be far more nuanced, intellectual and potentially radical than previously suggested.[3] Moreover, EBB's religious poetry is some of her most formally innovative and aesthetically intriguing and consequently demands serious attention in any consideration of her career.

EBB's religious commitments, as they are revealed in her extant correspondence, diary and autobiographical essays, are not easy to pin down or categorize for her relation to inherited religious ideas was always complicated. During her youth, EBB's family often attended the Anglican church near their home and yet they generally aligned themselves to a greater degree with the non-conformist, dissenting Congregationalists (also known as the Independents) who stood opposed to the established Tory Church of England and who were therefore associated with the Whig party that the Barrett family supported. In terms of doctrine, the Congregationalists, like many of the nonconformist sects connected with the late-eighteenth-century Evangelical revivals, were highly democratic, rejecting religious ceremonies, priesthoods and hierarchies, and emphasizing the individual's personal encounter with God. Indeed, as Mark Knight and Emma Mason note, the 'Church' of the Congregationalists 'only signified as far as it identified a living, gathered group of believers who had to take responsibility for their own faith by studying the Bible, acting charitably, and supporting their community.' Moreover, with no power invested in a ruling body, each congregation was self-regulating and each believer remained 'relatively free to speak his or her mind on matters of faith without fear of correction or derision.'[4]

This emphasis on spiritual autonomy and a personal relationship with the deity was central to EBB's religious thinking from an early stage. In 'Glimpses into My Own Life and Literary Character', for example, EBB notes that at the age of twelve she 'revolted at the idea of an established religion' and subsequently sought to develop a religion of her own, 'not the deep persuasion of the mild Christian but the wild visions of an enthusiast' (*Correspondence* 1:351). Whilst this is clearly galvanized in part by that testing of inherited ideas associated with puberty, the questioning of established religion suggested here would stay with her in one form or another throughout her life. Indeed, after realizing the error of her youthful 'wild visions', she nevertheless still amended her edition of *The Book of Common Prayer* so that it read 'Church *in* England' rather than 'Church *of* England' (*Correspondence* 1:352, n.14, my italics). Her faith was clearly not to be restricted to the state-endorsed institution.

A decade later, this commitment to spiritual openness is evident in EBB's extant diary of 1831-2, where she records her reading of religious texts as varied as the Greek Testament, Chrysostom's *Commentary on the Ephesians*, Bishop Jewel's *Apologia Ecclesiæ Anglicanæ*, Richard Hooker's *Discourse of Justification*, John Wesley's *Treatise*, and the works of John Bunyan. Moreover, her correspondence with Hugh Stuart Boyd from this period reveals her engagement with, and detailed understanding of, a range of key theological debates and issues, including the idea of Atonement, Calvinist doctrine, the role of the ancient Church fathers, and the push for Catholic emancipation. Consequently, EBB appears to have been increasingly drawn to what might be termed an inclusive, non-sectarian, broad-church outlook which can also be linked to her Whig beliefs in the civil liberties of the individual. For as she wrote to Boyd in 1834, she was 'weary of controversy in religion...The command is – not, "argue with one another." – but, "love one another." ...They who lie on the bosom of Jesus, must lie there TOGETHER!' (*Correspondence* 3:98). Indeed, a decade later, she would write to Robert Browning that no matter what walls might be built by 'exclusive religionists', 'there is only one church in heaven & earth, with one divine High Priest to it.' Hence her love of the Congregationalists, who 'know what the "liberty of Christ" *means*, far better than those do who call themselves "churchmen," – & stand altogether as a body, on higher ground' (*Correspondence* 11:10).

Interestingly, EBB's early poetry of the 1820s includes very few explicitly religious works. As I discussed in Chapter 1, her first major poem, *The Battle of Marathon*, deals with the pagan world of ancient Greece – a topic which, as I note below, EBB would return to and treat in a significantly different manner in *Poems* (1844) – whilst religious issues in *An Essay on Mind, and Other Poems* (1826) are limited to the rather undistinguished poem 'The Prayer' and the apocalyptic vision at the close of the more powerful 'The Dream: A Fragment' where the speaker laments the temporal world's tendency to turn away from God and emphasizes instead the need to stand before him 'face to face' (l.49).

In her volumes of the 1830s, however, EBB began to explore the possibilities of religious poetry with far more subtlety and experimentation, a fact which might be related, at least in part, to the private spiritual crisis engendered by the death of her mother in 1828. In a wider intellectual context, though, the 1830s was also a decade of increasing religious controversy on a variety of fronts. As the decade opened, for example, Charles Lyell published the first volume of his revolutionary text, *Principles of Geology* (3 vols, 1830–3), which promoted the uniformitarian doctrine that the earth has been subject to processes of continuous gradual change over millions of years. This was an argument which effectively substituted 'laws ... governing the material world' for the traditional view that the earth's structures were created by some 'mysterious and extraordinary agency' (God), and which consequently challenged the age of the world as suggested by the Bible.[5] (EBB explicitly mentions Boyd discussing 'the geological question' in a letter of September 1830: *Correspondence* 2:256.) In 1833, controversy also developed with the emergence of the Oxford Movement which sought to revive high doctrine and ceremonial in Church of England practices, thereby opposing liberal tendencies in the Church and galvanizing the shift to Anglo-Catholicism (the Movement would break down in 1845 when John Henry Newman, one of its key promoters, became a Catholic). And two years later, in 1835, this growing sense of religious instability was further deepened with the publication of David Strauss' *Das Leben Jesu*, a text which became central to the new rationalizing 'Higher Criticism' of the Bible through its rejection of the idea of the miracles and direct divine intervention. Significantly, therefore, EBB turns to writing her key religious poetry in an atmosphere of fierce public debate over spiritual matters.

In the short poems attached to the 1833 volume, *Prometheus Bound and Miscellaneous Poems*, EBB's speakers repeatedly look to God as a means of transcending the fragmented self in the modern world (as in 'A Sea-Side Meditation', 'A Vision of Life and Death' and 'Remonstrance') and begin to explore both the nature of the deity and the relations between the secular and the spiritual ('The Image of God', 'Idols', 'Weariness'). Further, in 'The Appeal', the speaker argues, in oddly (and somewhat problematic) imperialist language, that the children of England should '[s]hout aloud the words that free' (1.20) – that is, the Christian message of hope – to the populations of foreign nations as a means of combating crime, violence and war. Such key ideas concerning the tensions between this world and the next, sin and redemption, the mortal and the divine, are then interrogated in more detail in the larger 1838 collection in poems such as 'Isobel's Child', 'The Virgin Mary to the Child Jesus', 'The Mediator', 'The Weeping Saviour', and the fascinating 'The Soul's Travelling', in which God is proposed as the means of relieving both individual despair and the wider problems of the city with its 'beggar's whine', 'gin-door's oath', 'brothel shriek' and 'Newgate laugh' (ll.17; 29; 39) – an early concern with those 'Condition of England' debates which EBB would deal with more explicitly in 'The Cry of the Children' and *Aurora Leigh*.

It was with *The Seraphim*, however, the title poem of the 1838 volume, that EBB made her most significant development in the writing of religious poetry to date. For as Karen Deileman has detailed, in contrast to much of EBB's earlier poetry, such as her hymns in the 1833 volume, there appears to have been a conscious shift here to a much more intellectual and intricate consideration of theological issues which is derived, in part, from EBB's understanding of the more discursive nature of the sermons associated with her Congregationalist background. The result, as Deileman terms it, is 'a religious poetry of greater exposition' which, in works such as *The Seraphim* and *A Drama of Exile*, 'investigat[es] and expound[s] from new perspectives the essential stories of the Christian faith.'[6] Indeed, such revisionary strategies consequently saw EBB writing some of the most daring and original religious poetry of the first half of the nineteenth century.

The 'essential story' of *The Seraphim* is that of Christ's passion, a subject which, EBB notes in the preface, was initially suggested by her translation of *Prometheus Bound*. For had Æschylus lived later, she suggests, he would have rejected Prometheus as the subject of his work and focused on Christ instead, writing of 'the Victim, whose sustaining thought beneath an unexampled agony, was not the Titanic "I can revenge," but the celestial "I can forgive!"' (*Works* 4:289). EBB therefore takes over where Æschylus left off and her treatment of the subject is certainly highly innovative as she depicts the crucifixion through the eyes of two angels looking down on Golgotha from heaven. As she details in the preface, her aim here was to 'gather some vision of the supreme spectacle under a less usual aspect, – to glance at it, as dilated in seraphic eyes, and darkened and deepened by the near association with blessedness and Heaven.' Consequently, in order to attain this perspective, EBB depicts herself climbing up to heaven, 'endeavour[ing] to count some steps of the ladder at Bethel, – a very few steps, and as seen between the clouds' (*Works* 4:290–1). This is an image which, as I have noted elsewhere, interestingly suggests an attempt to achieve one of the most direct engagements with the divine possible, almost as if this is an extreme version of the Congregationalist idea of an unmediated relationship with God.[7] Moreover, it places the poet herself in heaven and seemingly on a level with the seraphim, the guardians of God's throne who occupy the highest position in Christian angelology. EBB clearly recognised that in taking on this particular subject and in adopting this particular stance she was pushing, as she wrote to Lady Margaret Cocks, 'near the precipice' of poetic decorum (*Correspondence* 3:276). And yet EBB was never one to let such concerns hold her back and the result was one of the most important poems of her career.

The originality of *The Seraphim* emerges not only from the perspective used, however, but also from the form, which EBB termed a hybrid 'dramatic lyric' (*Works* 4:290) – interestingly, the phrasing employed by Robert Browning four years later as the title of his new collection (*Dramatic Lyrics*, 1842). For this lengthy work, which occupies more than a thousand lines of verse, is constructed as an ongoing dialogue between the two seraphim,

Ador the Strong and Zerah the Bright One, which sees EBB, as Rebecca Stott has noted, playing with conversation and ventriloquism as a way of exploring different viewpoints.[8] This structure consequently enables EBB to put debate at the very heart of her poem – as she would with later works such as 'Lady Geraldine's Courtship' and *Aurora Leigh* – as she maps out the process of the angels' coming to intellectual and emotional awareness through their consideration of key spiritual issues such as the relations between heaven and earth, the meaning of existence, the incarnation, predestination, grace and forgiveness, the nature of sin, and the possibilities of salvation and redemption. It is an astute technique which demonstrates EBB's keen understanding of contemporary theological concerns and which clearly contributes to what Antony H. Harrison has termed the text's 'adventurous poetic strategies'.[9]

At the opening of the poem, Ador and Zerah are already in a position of isolation, having stayed back in a state of anxious indecision after the rest of the heavenly host has departed for Golgotha. Indeed, their 'inbetween' state is foregrounded here by their being depicted on the threshold between the heavenly and the temporal, on *'the outer side of the shut heavenly gate'* (*Works* 1:81). Like many of EBB's speakers and protagonists, the seraphim are effectively exiled from their home – their isolation is further compounded by the fact that they are fearful of looking back through heaven's gates in case they see God revealed in all his glory, 'the veil undone' (l.76) – and they are consequently forced to confront a disturbing new experience which will eventually lead to personal growth and greater understanding. Indeed, Zerah, who has never been to earth since it was in its prelapsarian state, is at first so terrified about what he might see of the world ('God-created and God-curst,/ Where man is, and the thorn', ll.140–1) that he can only bring himself to look at what is occurring through the reflections in Ador's eyes. For much of the poem, therefore, the frightened Zerah experiences events in mediated and distanced form (in a manner akin to the pre-fallen Lady of Shalott in Tennyson's poem), a situation which effectively emphasizes the idea of suffering associated with spiritual growth which underpins much of EBB's poetry.

In the second part of the poem, however, as Zerah finally

turns to look at the Crucifixion for himself, he comes to realise how his perception of the seraphim's heavenly home requires reassessment in the face of what he sees of the temporal world and man's emotional response to Christ's death:

> Heaven is dull
> Mine Ador, to man's earth. The light that burns
>> In fluent, refluent motion
>> Along the crystal ocean;
> The springing of the golden harps between
> The bowery wings, in fountains of sweet sound;
> The winding, wandering music that returns
> Upon itself, exultingly self-bound
> In the great spheric round
>> Of everlasting praises
>
> .   .   .   .   .
>
> My heaven! my home of heaven! my infinite
> Heaven-choirs! what are ye to this dust and death,
> This cloud, this cold, these tears, this failing breath,
> Where God's immortal love now issueth
>> In this MAN'S woe?

(ll.596–615)

As the poem focuses in on Christ's cross, then, there is an increased sense that a meaningful spiritual home is not to be found in the seemingly 'dull', 'self-bound' and 'ever-lasting' heaven which the seraphim occupy – a strikingly controversial argument – but rather with the 'God-orphaned' Christ (l.935) who, like Prometheus chained to the rock in EBB's 1833 translation, occupies a position of traditionally 'feminine' passivity.[10] Moreover, as Linda M. Lewis has emphasized, this scene of potential salvation is occupied by not one but two outcast figures. For at the base of the cross kneels the weeping Mary Magdalene, transferred from her marginalized position as outcast prostitute right into the very centre of the narrative of Christ's mission and resurrection. Indeed, as Lewis notes, it was Mary who carried the news of Christ's resurrection to the apostles in an act 'all the more remarkable, given that in Jewish culture of the time women were not allowed to bear legal witness, and this particular woman was tainted in reputation.'[11] Only through the exile figure, the poem suggests, can a meaningful spiritual home be found.

The Seraphim is therefore a potentially far more radical poem than Helen Cooper allows for when she reads it as one of EBB's 'exercises in orthodox religious thought.'[12] Moreover, as I have noted above, EBB was herself aware that her poem was 'near the precipice' in subject matter and treatment and consequently she strategically downplayed her challenge to decorum in the epilogue where she asks in her own voice:

> ...what am I
> To counterfeit, with faculty earth-darkened,
> Seraphic brows of light
> And seraph language never used nor harkened?'

(ll.1019–22)

Certainly, on initial publication many contemporary reviewers were clearly cautious about the work, with *The Athenaeum*, for example, lamenting EBB's lack of 'discriminating taste' and the *Examiner* suggesting that she was 'in danger of being spoiled by over-ambition, and...realizing no greater or more final reputation than a heretical one' (*Correspondence* 4:375). Nevertheless, EBB would continue to experiment with religious poetry and to explore the relations between the exile figure and a perceived spiritual home for the rest of her career. Indeed, the lead poem to *Poems* (1844), the generically-innovative and revisionary *A Drama of Exile*, saw her taking this experimentation to even greater lengths and with astonishing results.

Significantly, EBB's *Poems* was published in the same year as Robert Chambers' controversial *Vestiges of the Natural History of Creation*, a work which argued for an evolutionary model of development and consequently challenged both the 'natural' order and God's centrality in the universe, thereby paving the way for the publication of Darwin's *Origin of Species* fifteen years later. The early 1840s therefore continued the atmosphere of religious controversy and debate of the 1830s, and in many ways *A Drama of Exile* contributes to this debate in its own way. For here EBB rehearses the Biblical narrative of the expulsion from Eden but from Eve's perspective rather than Adam's, thus enabling her, as she wrote to her friend Richard Hengist Horne, to offer a more generous understanding of Eve's role, to articulate previously silenced voices, and to rescript conventional prejudices: '*"First in the transgression"* has been said over

& over again, because of the tradition, – but *first & deepest in the sorrow*, nobody seems to have said, or, at least, written of, as conceiving' (*Correspondence* 8:117). Moreover, as EBB boldly states in the preface to the poem, this was a task which she felt women poets were particularly qualified to undertake (*Works* 2:567). For in reconstructing the fall from this perspective, EBB is, of course, also rewriting the androcentric tradition of Biblical epic as constructed by John Milton in his great poem, *Paradise Lost* (1667; revised ed. 1674), the patriarchal and misogynistic lines of which many nineteenth-century women writers sought to challenge.[13] Beginning 'A Drama of Exile' where *Paradise Lost* ends, therefore, and shifting the focus to the *consequences* of the fall, EBB undertakes what Marjorie Stone terms a 'de-centering' of Milton.[14] And yet interestingly, in the preface EBB also suggests that her own position in what we would now term the literary canon, in contrast to Milton, is that of the outsider: 'He [Milton] should be within, I thought, with his Adam and Eve unfallen or falling, – and I, without, with my EXILES, – *I* also an exile!' (*Works* 2:568). Consequently, she purposefully aligns herself with the fallen Eve but, given the poem's narrative, this is a position which has the subversive potential to be *en*abling rather than *dis*-abling.

EBB defined *A Drama of Exile* as 'a sort of Masque...in blank verse, with lyrics interspersed' (*Correspondence* 8:84). Certainly the work is generically complex, involving, like *The Seraphim*, little action but rather centring upon a series of conversations and confrontations between the newly-fallen Adam and Eve, Lucifer, an array of angels and spirits who act as a version of the traditional Greek chorus, and, finally, Christ. It is a structure which, in another parallel with *The Seraphim*, allows for reflection and debate upon a host of theological issues, including the nature of post-lapsarian existence ('that web of pain', 1.566), the idea of free will, the problem of defining fallen humans ('earth-angel or earth-demon', 1.157), concepts of beauty, typology and prefiguring, and the complexities of blame and forgiveness. Much space is given to Lucifer's speeches as he mocks Adam and Eve for their naivety, reflects upon his own fall from grace, and defines himself as the archetypal exile, 'struck out from nature in a blot,/ The outcast and the mildew of things good,/ The leper of angels' (ll.1387–9). In many ways, then, the poem offers a very different Lucifer from that celebrated by the (male) Romantic poets such as Shelley and Byron.

Yet the major concern in *A Drama of Exile* is rather with the *human* protagonists who are first seen, again as with the protagonists of *The Seraphim*, occupying a threshold space, located on 'the outer side of the gate of Eden shut fast with cloud' and fearful of looking back at their now lost home (*Works* 1:10). The narrative subsequently interrogates their self-development, as Adam revokes his status as 'king' of Eden and refuses to allocate blame for the fall. Eve asks him to condemn and cast her out, but instead he asserts that she herself is his Eden, his 'best gift' (1.462) when all other gifts have passed away. Moreover, he proceeds to celebrate their kiss as a new sacred act. In EBB's version of the narrative, then, Adam radically overturns inherited belief by arguing that it is he, not Eve, who is 'deepest in the guilt,/ If last in the transgression' (ll.458–9).

As EBB's preface indicates, however, it is by placing the principal focus on Eve that the key possibilities for revisioning the fall are engendered. For whilst Adam clearly seeks to offer models of support for Eve, it is she, newly fallen into experience and thereby 'schooled by sin' (1.1182), who teaches him patience and acceptance and she who first steps out into the desert of the post-lapsarian world. (EBB would repeatedly employ the trope of a woman determined to walk alone into a new situation as a signifier of potential empowerment, as seen in the later *Aurora Leigh*.) Moreover, as the poem is keen to emphasize, Eve will become the mother of future generations ('My seed, my seed/ There is hope set on THEE', ll.1747–8), thereby occupying a position of redemptive and transformative possibility which is reinforced by the vision of Christ promising 'a new Eden-gate' that will 'open on a hinge of harmony/ And let you through to mercy' (ll.1990–2). The final scene of the poem, therefore, which almost suggests the notion of the *felix culpa* ('fortunate fall'), is one of hope as Adam and Eve go out into the world with the angelic chorus singing '*Exiled is not lost*' (1.2258). Temporal Eden might be forsaken, figured in an echo of *The Seraphim* as 'not new created but new cursed' (1.58), but the result is a revisioning of the world and the promise of new life since, beyond death, a spiritual home may be attainable with Christ in heaven.

As Karen Dieleman has suggested, both *The Seraphim* and *A Drama of Exile* constitute attempts to come to religious understanding 'through hesitant, confused, wondering, fearful, yet worshipful speakers.'[15] Certainly, *A Drama of Exile* in particular was to influence a number of later women poets, such as Christina Rossetti, who also sought to rewrite the Biblical narrative of Eve along similar revisionary and empathetic lines.[16] Yet the hope of religious salvation which these poems eventually embrace was not always to be easily attained by EBB's protagonists. For as I explore in Chapter 4, political poems such as 'The Cry of the Children' and 'The Runaway Slave at Pilgrim's Point' overtly question the ways in which religious ideas can be manipulated to uphold oppressive and alienating power structures. And in a poem added to the 1850 edition of *Poems*, 'Human Life's Mystery', EBB once again shows belief to be far from unproblematic. Indeed, this poem – which interestingly echoes the religious doubt expressed in parts of Tennyson's great spiritual diary, *In Memoriam*, published the same year – is shot through with anxiety concerning the relationship between the secular and sacred worlds and deploys language and imagery which places an ambivalent emphasis on the notion of trust:

> The senses folding thick and dark
>   About the stifled soul within,
> We guess diviner things beyond,
> And yearn to them with yearning fond;
> We strike out blindly to a mark
>   Believed in, but not seen.

(ll.7–12)

Here the speaker's anxiety is caught in the use of the phrases 'We *guess*' and 'Believed in, *but not seen*' (my emphasis). For as the poem proceeds to suggest, 'God keeps his holy mysteries/ Just on the outside of man's dream' (ll.25–6), seemingly another instance of potential exclusion as in *The Seraphim* and *The Drama of Exile*. Consequently, we have to trust blindly in God's existence and the holy sanctuary which might be offered us after death. Indeed, recalling the repeated articulation of the distance between humans and God which occurs in much metaphysical poetry – a body of work which, although EBB questioned the classification, she nevertheless celebrated in her 1842 essays on the history of poetry (*Works* 4:468–9) – we 'grope' for reassurance of God's benevolence, 'stretch[ing] our hands abroad.../...in our agony' (ll.57–8). It is significant, therefore, that when EBB published this poem, she placed it next to 'A Child's Thoughts of God', a work which emphasizes the child's instinctive belief in God despite the lack of visible evidence and which equates God's embrace throbbing through the universe with a mother kissing her child. Such is the trust we need to have, EBB implies, if we are to achieve redemption.

At the end of volume two of *Poems* (1844), and therefore the close to the collection that opens with *A Drama of Exile*, EBB placed what has become one of her most popular and widely-anthologized poems, 'The Death of Pan'. This is a remarkable work, celebrating the moment of Christ's death as the concurrent point of the death of all those pagan deities who, after being described in luxurious and bacchanalian detail clearly designed to suggest their seductiveness, are shown to be 'discrowned and desecrated,/ Disinherited of thunder' (ll.157–8). Dismissing the ancient gods which had attracted her in her youthful reading and which she employed in *The Battle of Marathon*, EBB emphasizes instead a new aesthetic where poets should '[l]ook up Godward' and 'speak the truth in/ Worthy song from earnest soul!' (ll.269–70).[17] As the preface to *The Seraphim* volume indicates, however, this is a position which EBB had herself been adopting for years, even if – or maybe because – the ways of the soul are complex, challenging and difficult. For as her poetry repeatedly suggests, some kind of spiritual or religious belief is a crucial component in EBB's notion of a secure 'home', particularly when, as the following chapters demonstrate, a home in the temporal world based on an emotional relationship or political security is usually so difficult to attain.

39

3

The Search for an Emotional Home

In the last chapter I explored some of EBB's key religious poems from the 1830s and 1840s as a means of starting to consider her protagonists' search for the security of a home through spiritual belief. Whilst EBB was always cautious about institutionalized religion – the year before she died, for example, she wrote to her friend Eliza Ogilvy that 'We want a blast of free air through the churches, & a sweeping away of traditional forms' (*Ogilvy* 169) – she nevertheless maintained a strong spiritual commitment throughout her life and saw the role of the poet, at least in part, to be dedicated to the revelation of God's truth. In poems such as *The Seraphim* and *A Drama of Exile*, therefore, she depicts faith in Christ as offering the hope of ultimate salvation even if the protagonists of the poems are in outcast or alienated positions or, as with the speaker of 'Human Life's Mystery', implicitly questioning of God's existence.

As Glennis Stephenson has suggested, however, EBB's poems often 'challenge the idea that God's love alone can provide happiness.'[1] In this chapter, then, I turn to consider the search of EBB's speakers for a home or place of security in the *temporal* world through human love and emotional engagement. EBB returned repeatedly to consideration of what love meant and how a meaningful relationship between individuals could be established and maintained, although the complexities of this consideration have often been misread or elided through the mythologizing process which transformed EBB herself into the protagonist of one of literary history's most famous romances. The narrative of her clandestine marriage to Robert Browning and their fleeing the draconian rule of her father to start a new life, both personal and professional, in Italy has been rehearsed time and again – most famously in Rudolph Besier's 1931 play, *The Barretts of Wimpole Street* and the subsequent 1934 film. Moreover, this narrative has often tended to reduce EBB to the roles of oppressed daughter and 'rescued' wife, and her powerful poetry to a single line from *Sonnets from the Portuguese*: 'How do I love thee? Let me count the ways' (Sonnet 43, 1.1).

In the last two decades, however, a significant shift in understanding has occurred as a number of critics, including Glennis Stephenson, Angela Leighton, Marjorie Stone and Rebecca Stott, have worked to debunk this overbearing mythology by offering sophisticated analyses of EBB's poems which reveal many of them to be highly critical of the prevailing nineteenth-century notions of love and heterosexual relationships, rather than unquestioningly supportive of them.[2] Indeed, in an oft-quoted comment concerning the reaction of Edward Barrett, EBB's father, to his children's relationships – he famously forbade any of his offspring to marry and when three of them did (Elizabeth in 1846, Henrietta in 1850 and Alfred in 1855), he subsequently disowned them and cut off all contact – EBB astutely argued that the blame was not to be laid exclusively with her father or any individual, but was rather embedded in dominant socio-political structures: the 'evil', as she termed it, is 'in the system' (*Correspondence* 11:43). And it is this 'system' of prescribed expectations and inherited structures of familial, matrimonial and sexual relationships which EBB's poetry interrogates in one form or another across her career. Indeed, Aurora's words to Romney on the subject of love might equally serve to reveal EBB's own position:

> I would not be a woman like the rest,
> A simple woman who believes in love
> And owns the right of love because she loves,
> And, hearing she's beloved, is satisfied
> With what contents God: I must analyse,
> Confront, and question...

> (*Aurora Leigh*, 9:660–5)

In the following discussions, then, I focus upon a number of EBB's poems taken predominantly from the 1830s and 1840s which 'analyse', 'confront' and 'question' emotional relationships in this way, and argue that whilst EBB repeatedly explores love as a potential solution to her speakers' quest for a secure home in the world, these explorations often reveal love and relationships to be unsatisfactory and anxiety-ridden at best and, indeed, sometimes brutally destructive.

Interestingly, in EBB's early work, such as that incorporated in *An Essay on Mind, and Other Poems* (1826), love tends to be presented in a positive manner as both supportive and central to the structures of EBB's childhood family, with poems such as 'To My Father on His Birth-Day' and 'Verses to My Brother' celebrating the 'days of pleasant mirth' at Hope End ('To My Father', l.1). By the mid-1830s, however, a new overtly-critical edge enters much of EBB's writing on relationships as the poet matures and begins to question the socio-political constructs and frameworks which determine, shape and, in many cases, restrict emotional and sexual engagement. In the 1838 volume, *The Seraphim, and Other Poems*, for example, EBB includes two poems, 'The Romaunt of Margret' and 'A Romance of the Ganges', which are key to this developing critique and which draw upon the ballad form that EBB appears to have found particularly suitable for this kind of socio-political intervention. EBB's ballads were extremely popular in her own day and drew upon the revival of the form initiated by poets such as Burns, Wordsworth and Scott. With their strong narrative lines, psychological complexity, and depiction of scenes of conflict and tension in often historicized settings, the revived ballads marked a shift in poetic approach, as EBB specifically high-lighted in her 1842 essays on the history of poetry. For as she notes, using images of revolution and liberation, the ballad revival engendered 'the putting down of the Dryden dynasty, the breaking of the serf bondage, [and] the wrenching of the iron from the soul' (*Works* 4:477). Yet whilst EBB's own ballads were highly influential on subsequent poets such as Christina Rossetti and Dante Gabriel Rossetti, they were largely dismissed by many twentieth-century critics for their perceived naivety and what Alethea Hayter claimed was a saccharine taste like 'custard and crystallized violets'.[3] Only relatively recently have critics such as Dorothy Mermin, Glennis Stephenson and, most extensively, Marjorie Stone started to unpack the often subversive gender performances and power politics at play within these poems and to reconsider the ways in which they both work within and undermine inherited conventions. Certainly, EBB's ballads are now being read as far more complicated, challenging and linguistically slippery in their interrogation of the socio-political construction of relationships than previously recognized.

EBB's first key ballad, 'The Romaunt of Margret' – the title of which points to the poem's participation within a pseudo-archaic tradition and which might also draw upon the subtitle of Byron's *Childe Harold's Pilgrimage: A Romaunt* – is a fascinating and bizarre work, utilizing that medieval-type setting typical of many early-nineteenth-century ballads with its references to the courtly paraphernalia of knights and ladies, hunts and battles, ancient halls and the feudal system. Opening with a frametale structure where the speaker, a minstrel-like figure, reaches for his/her harp and starts to sing, the poem narrates the story of Margret who is challenged by her own shadow, rising from the river by which she sits, to name somebody who truly loves her. The poem's tone therefore shifts quickly here from pastoral to gothic, a mode which fascinated EBB[4] and which, through its emphasis on what Rosemary Jackson terms 'the underside of realism', works both to expose that which individuals or society generally would rather repress and to write large the brutality of dominant socio-political structures.[5] Indeed, as Eugenia DeLamotte suggests in *Perils of the Night*, her insightful account of nineteenth-century women's gothic writing, gothic's 'focus on the most private demons of the psyche can never be separated from the persistent preoccupation with the social realities from which those demons always, in some measure, take their shape.'[6]

Certainly, in this poem such established social realities constantly fail Margret. For whilst she names the key members of her family for whom she has cared and denied herself in the past, the shadow takes on increasingly demonic form as it exposes the true nature of her relations with her brother, sister, father and lover. Her brother prefers the wine and song Margret provides to Margret herself; her sister prefers the golden comb and flowers she has given her; her father prefers his ancestral pile to any social relation whatsoever; and her last hope, her lover, although faithful to her when alive, now lies dead with

'the death-worm to his heart' and '[t]he wild hawk's bill...
dabbl[ing] still/ I' the mouth that vowed thee true' (ll.215; 211–
12). In this final indignity, the emotively-charged and symbo-
lically-resonant parts of the lover's body, the mouth and the
heart, are violated, decaying and depicted through a set of
images which, as in much war poetry, undercuts that conven-
tional celebration of the body, the *blazon*, found in traditional
love poetry.

The overpowering shadow in this poem is therefore evidently
meant to function, as in much gothic literature, as an
embodiment of Margret's repressed anxieties concerning not
only familial relations – 'the dark underside of family affection',
as Dorothy Mermin phrases it[7] – but also the nature of love and
sexuality more generally and her own identity and position in
the world in particular. This is certainly reinforced by the
increasing emphasis on the stagnation and decay of the physical
topography surrounding Margret, which serves as a projection
of her *psychological* landscape as she becomes undeniably aware
of the lack of a meaningful relationship in her life. For as
DeLamotte argues, 'the perils of the soul in its darkest night'
always work to 'reflect, in magnified and revealing forms, the
quotidian realities of life in the daylit world.'[8] The strategy of
nightmarish doubling in EBB's ballad thus foregrounds the
cruel disparity between perception and reality, and conse-
quently, in anguish at her isolation and sense of her life
revolving around an absent centre, Margret drowns herself:

> Her face was on the ground –
> None saw the agony.
> But the men at sea did that night agree
> They heard a drowning cry.
> And when the morning brake,
> Fast rolled the river's tide,
> With the green trees waving overhead,
> And a white corse laid beside.
> Margret, Margret.
>
> (ll.218–26)

Here, the continued 'fast roll[ing]' of the tide and the ceaseless
'waving' of the trees only serve to highlight the overriding *in*-
significance of Margret's death to an unconcerned world.
Indeed, the repeated refrain, 'Margret, Margret', used through-

44

out seems to suggest the progressive loss of the self which leaves only a mournful echo. But whilst the narrative of the poem might eventually silence the singer/speaker – in the last paragraph s/he returns the harp to its resting place – the final 'moral', with its emphasis on the falseness of 'failing human love' (l.240), clearly indicates that Margret is not the first, and certainly will not be the last, to suffer betrayal in this way.

This sense of betrayal and the dark underside of relationships also resonates throughout the other ballad of the *Seraphim* volume, the more famous 'A Romance of the Ganges', one of the poems which EBB originally wrote for Mary Russell Mitford's literary annual, *Findens' Tableaux*.[9] Commissioned to accompany a picture of 'a very charming group of Hindoo girls floating their lamps upon the Ganges', which reflects what Mitford termed a 'pretty superstition' (*Correspondence* 3:252), the resulting poem is anything but 'charming' or 'pretty' with its exposure of networks of treachery and perfidy. Indeed, 'A Romance of the Ganges' is a powerful tale of rivalry and revenge which, as Virginia Radley accurately notes, is 'injected ... with the kind of realism that is so characteristic of [EBB's] later poems of social protest'.[10] Consequently, it is very different to the gothicism of 'The Romaunt of Margret' in style, if not necessarily in message.

The poem opens at the riverside with Luti and Nuleeni releasing floating lamps onto the water as symbols of their respective loves. This explicit reliance on what EBB terms 'symbols low' (l.42) as a means of attempting to understand the complexities of relationships underlines many of the ballads, and here, as Luti watches, the light on her boat is extinguished, confirming that her lover has been false. Luti knows that her lover has been stolen away by her friend and consequently, as the light on Nuleeni's boat continues to shine, Luti, 'her eyes dilated wild' (l.183), demands two specific vows from her: firstly, that Nuleeni will remind her new husband of his infidelity on their wedding day (*'There is one betrays,/ While Luti suffers woe'*, ll.161–2); and, secondly, that Nuleeni will tell her future son of his father's wrong (significantly it is the *male* offspring that Luti believes needs instructing). Luti therefore seeks revenge by inserting into Nuleeni's family unit the tale of betrayal initiated by the false lover. Yet the notion of the family as it is represented in this poem is complex on several levels. For the place where

Luti stands by the river in order to confirm her lover's faithlessness is also the place where she lost her 'loving father':

> I do remember watching
> Beside this river-bed,
> When on my childish knee was laid
> My dying father's head
>
> (ll.73–6)

The riverside is therefore associated with multiple losses which leaves Luti, like Margret, deprived of both familial and romantic relationships. Subsequently, in her despair, she too drowns herself, seemingly in an attempt to return to the loving relations she associates with her dead father. In the world of 'A Romance of the Ganges', then, as in that of 'The Romaunt of Margret', relationships seem trapped in a continuous cycle of false hope and inevitable betrayal with the only way out appearing to be self-annihilation.

As Dorothy Mermin has astutely argued, EBB's ballads, like many of her other poems of the 1830s and 1840s, 'offer a covert but thorough-going reassessment, often a total repudiation, of the Victorian ideas about womanliness to which they ostensibly appeal'.[11] Certainly they serve time and again to expose the heavy burden placed upon women in terms of gender expectations and family responsibilities and to sharply critique what Marjorie Stone terms 'the "female plots" shaping women's lives'.[12] Interestingly, however, the poem placed next to 'A Romance of the Ganges' in The Seraphim, and Other Poems, the thirty-stanza lyric work, 'An Island', offers a very different depiction of relationships based on positive understanding and the development of a meaningful 'home' – even if, as the first noun of the poem indicates, this is solely a 'dream'. For here EBB offers one of her most detailed descriptions of natural landscape in a vision of 'an island place' (l.1) which is almost arcadian or prelapsarian in its beauty and abundance of 'heavenly trees and flowers and fruits' (l.24). Indeed, there is often a sustained, almost Keatsian sensuality in the evocations here:

> The place is all awave with trees,
> Limes, myrtles purple-beaded,
> Acacias having drunk the lees
> Of the night-dew, faint-headed,

And wan, grey olive-woods, which seem
The fittest foliage for a dream.

(ll.31–6)

As the speaker continues to affirm, this is an environment where all creatures live in harmony, where there is no evidence of fear or threat ('No guns nor springes in my dream', she notes, l.84), and where systems of control and authority are significantly absent (she is keen to emphasize that the sheep are 'unruled by shepherds', for example, l.76). And it is in this version of 'Dante's paradise', as the speaker terms it (l.20), that she imagines establishing an alternative social reality as she builds a community with two or three others who similarly seek to reject 'Man's veering heart and careless eyes' and commit themselves instead to 'Nature's steadfast sympathies' (ll.113–14). Interestingly, the seemingly-loaded emphasis on 'Man' here, in contrast to the traditionally feminine Nature with her 'sympathies' and 'faithfulness' (l.115), suggests that the speaker's dream is more than a desire to escape mankind generally and might rather be a dream of a single-sex, proto-feminist separatist community – a reading which would sit persuasively with the general critique of heterosexual relations in this volume overall. Indeed, the speaker specifically states that her vision of a new social order, which rejects the dominant economic and utilitarian concerns of the early nineteenth century, will also preclude the suffering and betrayal associated with the female protagonists in the ballads: 'We cannot say by stream or shade,/ "I suffered *here*, – was *here* betrayed"', she notes in what appears a direct echo of the imagery of both 'The Romaunt of Margret' and 'A Romance of the Ganges' (ll.131–2). Instead, the speaker envisages herself being dedicated to art and poetry and even imagines developing a new language which is associated with a past golden age – '[s]ounds sweet as Hellas spake in youth' (l.147). The poem therefore seems to offer nothing less than a vision of a new utopia (both ecological and proto-feminist) and a potential ideal home which is marked by harmony, equality and commitment to art. Moreover, like other literary utopias, it consequently works both to expose the problems with the 'real', everyday world and to foreground the political potential of what could be brought into being. For whilst the world of 'An Island' might only be a dream and therefore impossible to

47

sustain, EBB is able to use this imagined community, as with the alternative 'worlds' in the ballads, to deconstruct and subtly challenge established ideas concerning love, heterosexual relations and structures of power, and thereby envisage a more meaningful notion of 'home'.

EBB was to continue her interrogation of love and heterosexual relationships as part of the quest for a meaningful home in her next collection, *Poems* (1844), where the notion of dealing with woman's 'alloted grief' (*Works* 2:567) which EBB highlights in relation to the key poem, *A Drama of Exile*, is further explored in the two key ballads, 'The Romance of the Swan's Nest' and 'The Romaunt of the Page'. The first of these, which initially appears the slighter of the two in complexity, focuses on the figure of Little Ellie who, like Margret, is depicted as a solitary female sitting by a stream. Once again, therefore, water – which in nineteenth-century literature has various symbolic connotations of imagination, creativity and sexuality – becomes the site of introspection and potential new awareness. But instead of confronting her own destructive shadow as Margret does, Little Ellie, rocking herself in a childish, self-indulgent motion, dreams of her future lover who, she imagines, will fulfill her desires of a chivalrous relationship:

> Little Ellie in her smile
> Chooses...'I will have a lover,
> Riding on a steed of steeds!
> He shall love me without guile,
> And to *him* I will discover
> The swan's nest among the reeds.'
>
> (ll.19–24)

Abandoning herself to a fantasy of being swept off her feet, in a parody of standard fairy-tale narratives, Ellie here promises to exchange her lover's devotion for a view of '[t]he swan's nest among the reeds'. Yet, after extensive musings on the details of her future life, which interestingly cast her repeatedly in a position of power over her lover, Ellie's dream is shattered when she returns to the nest itself:

> Pushing through the elm-tree copse,
> Winding up the stream, light-hearted,
> Where the osier pathway leads –

> Past the boughs she stoops – and stops.
> Lo, the wild swan had deserted –
> And a rat had gnawed the reeds.
>
> (ll.91–6)

As with 'A Romance of the Ganges', then, 'The Romance of the Swan's Nest' centres on a sign, a 'symbol low' ('Ganges', l.42), which requires interpretation. But here the meaning of the desecrated nest in the middle of the otherwise pastoral environment is particularly difficult to pin down since the swan, a bird which is known for mating for life, has abandoned the scene and seemingly left its eggs, the symbol of potential new life, to be destroyed by the rat. It is a brutal scenario but as critics such as Angela Leighton and Helen Cooper have suggested, the nest has wider, and more disturbing, associations in its suggestiveness of Ellie's own sexuality.[13] In this reading, Ellie's fantasy of the chivalric knightly lover is replaced by a horrifying intimation of sexual violation and desertion, an interpretative pattern which sits tellingly alongside the narratives of betrayal running through the other ballads. Indeed, it then seems highly significant that Ellie's initial vision of her lover makes an ominous near-equation of love, possible sex, and murder since 'the lute he plays upon,/ Shall strike ladies into trouble,/ As his sword strikes men to death' (ll.28-30). Such is the likely outcome of delusional dreaming on courtly love, the poem appears to affirm.

The other key ballad of *Poems* (1844), 'The Romaunt of the Page', similarly works to expose the harsh realities of inherited chivalric values. Here the page of the title is a newly-wedded wife who follows her knight-husband to the Holy Wars in Palestine, dressing in disguise so that he believes her to be the dutiful male servant who subsequently saves his life in battle three times: 'Thou fearest not to steep in blood/ The curls upon thy brow', he unwittingly tells her (ll.9-10). Taking advantage of the fact that, due to their overly-hasty marriage, her husband has not seen her face, the page/wife is then able to question her husband on his understanding of both the institution of marriage and the nature of love, only to be horrified by his replies. For in reaction to the page's fabricated story of 'his' sister who followed her lover to the battlefield, the husband asserts that if his wife came after him to war, he could no longer think of them as married and would rather consider her '[u]nwomaned' and therefore only 'my servitor' (ll.196; 228). It is highly ironic, then, that the poem ends with the page saving her knight-husband's life one more time as she urges him to safety and feels the 'scimitar gleam down' on herself in his stead (l.323).

As Marjorie Stone has argued, in this poem EBB 'employs the starker power structures of medieval society to foreground the status of women as objects in a male economy of social exchange'.[14] It is therefore intriguing that 'The Romaunt of the Page', like 'A Romance of the Ganges', was written for Mitford's Findens' Tableaux, where it was published in an edition subtitled 'A Series of Picturesque Illustrations of the Womanly Virtues'. Clearly, the poem appears to undercut the ideological sugges-tions of its place of publication since it repeatedly exposes the limitations and double standards of 'womanly virtues' as they are prescribed within dominant culture and rehearsed by the knight/husband's rhetoric. For whilst the knight might prefer to think of his wife at home veiled and attending chapel, it is she who takes on the heroic role and repeatedly saves his life in a manner which his reactionary views would condemn. Further-more, although the page's annihilation is seemingly inevitable, like that of Margret and Luti, the emphasis throughout the poem lies on her autonomy and her effectiveness in 'the bloody battle-game' (l.16). Certainly, her death is constructed as far more honourable and purposeful than the deaths of the other, more conventional women whose bodies litter this poem – the page's own mother who significantly dies during her daughter's marriage service, and the abbess from the isolated convent on the island in the sea whose death is lamented by her nuns via the repeated dirge refrain. Consequently, in many ways the poem that EBB termed in a letter to Hugh Stuart Boyd 'a very long barbarous ballad...containing a Ladye dressed up like a page & galloping off to Palestine in a manner that would scandalise' (Correspondence 4:33; 42) might be read as a study in possible modes of resistance to both the dominant social order and received gender expectations.

In her ground-breaking study of EBB's contribution to a developing tradition of Victorian women's poetry which 'writes against the heart', Angela Leighton has argued that EBB perceives love 'not as a conclusive emotional absolute, but as a mixture of lust, ambition, rhetoric, fear and, above all, conventionality.'[15] Certainly this reading is sustained by the range of poems I have examined so far, as it is by a number of other works in *Poems* (1844), such as 'Bertha in the Lane', 'A Lady's Yes', 'Change Upon Change', 'A Year's Spinning' and 'A Man's Requirements', texts which similarly expose the patterns of betrayal at the heart of the family, the brutal undercurrents in love relations, the inconsistency and transience of men's affections ('*I* will love *thee* – half-a-year – /As a man is able', says the male speaker of 'A Man's Requirements', ll.43-4), and the dominant ideologies and structures of society which support and inherently promote this gender imbalance. Whilst the female protagonists in these poems might only be able to challenge convention to a limited degree, if at all, and often end up dead at the text's close, the body of poetry overall nevertheless highlights the problems to do with the ideological work of both familial and heterosexual relations that EBB is adamant society needs to address. The quest for a secure home through emotional engagement consequently appears here to be as illusory as ever.

Significantly, it was only in the final poem that EBB wrote in order to equalize the length of the two volumes of *Poems* (1844), 'Lady Geraldine's Courtship', that she found a new set of mechanisms for addressing women's engagement with love and emotional relationships in a more positive light. For this poem, whilst still classified as a 'Romance' in the subtitle, is significantly 'A Romance of the Age' where EBB forsakes the pseudo-medieval or fairy-tale-like settings of her previous romance-ballads in favour of her own contemporary period. Indeed, this is the poem, EBB later noted, which inspired her to start work on the epic poem of modern society which would become *Aurora Leigh* and it is certainly a remarkable and innovative prototype in many ways. Composed in epistolary form, with the lowly poet Bertram writing to his friend about the aristocratic Geraldine, the poem first establishes and then demolishes many of the traditional courtly love conventions as Bertram laments how Geraldine appears far beyond his reach:

I was only a poor poet, made for singing at her casement,
As the finches or the thrushes, while she thought of other things.
Oh, she walked so high above me, she appeared to my abasement,

51

In her lovely silken murmur, like an angel clad in wings!

(ll.17–20)

Repeatedly placing himself in the position of spurned lover and deploying, as Glennis Stephenson notes, 'images commonly associated with love-melancholy',[16] Bertram finds it difficult to reconcile his imagined relationship with Geraldine – he constantly constructs her as a mythological deity, angel or temptress – with life in the modern world. For as 'the palpitating engines snort in steam' across Geraldine's estate (l.11), Bertram attacks the Victorian notion of progress in this 'wondrous age' (l.202), a notion which, he argues in an echo of Thomas Carlyle, prioritises industrial processes over the soul and the imagination (l.197–212). And yet it is precisely the modernity of the age and Geraldine's embracing of it which enables a positive outcome of the poem's emotional conflict. For Geraldine rejects the traditional passivity of woman which is embodied at its most extreme in the statue of Silence at the centre of the woods on her estate, and moves instead to a position of active speaking subject, confirming her agency and disregard of conventions by forming a cross-class relationship with Bertram. Indeed, the possessive in the title of the poem, 'Lady Geraldine's Courtship', seems to signify an interpretative shift here from the courtship *of* Geraldine to that courtship *by* Geraldine which would have been impossible in the inherited framework of the courtly love tradition or EBB's own earlier ballads.

Clearly, EBB recognized the subversive nature of 'Lady Geraldine's Courtship', writing to Hugh Stuart Boyd in July 1844 that her new poem deals with 'railroads, routes, & all manner of "temporalities," – and in so radical a temper, that I expect to be reproved for it by the conservative reviews round' (*Correspondence* 9:65). As this phrasing suggests, in many ways the poem functions as an intervention into those contemporary 'Condition of England' debates which EBB would explore in more detail in 'The Cry of the Children' and *Aurora Leigh*, but by placing it as the closing work to the first volume of *Poems* (1844), she also sought to resolve some of the problems around the representation of love and sex which she had been interrogating for the past decade. Significantly, too, it would be the reference to Robert Browning's work in 'Lady Geraldine's Courtship' –

Geraldine and Bertram read 'from Browning some "Pomegranate", which, if cut deep down the middle,/ Shows a heart within blood-tinctured, of a veined humanity' (ll.163–4) – which would initiate the great relationship of her own life.[17] And it was this relationship, of course, which then famously galvanized the writing of the astonishing *Sonnets from the Portuguese*, that series of poems where EBB once again showed how a meaningful relationship and a secure home could be structured through equality in love. Detailed treatment of this sequence is beyond the scope of this chapter and many critics, such as Helen Cooper, Glennis Stephenson, Dorothy Mermin, Marjorie Stone, Barbara Neri and Joseph Phelan, have insightfully explored its intricacies.[18] But it is important to note here the fundamental links between *Sonnets from the Portuguese* and 'Lady Geraldine's Courtship'. For as Alison Chapman observes, with this sequence EBB effectively transformed the sonnet tradition 'into a more muscular and dynamic poetics' in which she gave the speaking voice back to the previously-silenced woman who then repeatedly, and radically, claims equality with the man.[19] The traditional beloved subsequently becomes the lover in many of the poems, thereby collapsing the established boundaries between active and passive, male and female, reserve and passion, and effectively charting, as Isobel Armstrong argues, 'the struggle of the feminine subject to take up a new position which is free of dependency.'[20] This struggle is carefully mapped out across the sequence as the speaker variously questions the arrival of love and her worthiness of it; gradually accepts love's reality; examines her residual doubt; realizes that '[t]he face of all the world is changed' since love arrived (Sonnet 7, l.1); affirms her commitment to her lover; celebrates both a meeting of minds and potential bodily eroticism; seemingly rejects spiritual love for the earthly; and crucially comes to recognize that the beloved has the potential to offer a new home to replace that which has been lost:

> If I leave all for thee, wilt thou exchange
> And be all to me? Shall I never miss
> Home-talk and blessing and the common kiss
> That comes to each in turn, nor count it strange,
> When I look up, to drop on a new range
> Of walls and floors...another home than this?

Nay, wilt thou fill that place by me which is
Filled by dead eyes too tender to know change?
That's hardest. If to conquer love, has tried,
To conquer grief, tries more...as all things prove;
For grief indeed is love and grief beside.
Alas, I have grieved so I am hard to love.
Yet love me – wilt thou? Open thy heart wide,
And fold within, the wet wings of thy dove.

(Sonnet 35)

In this poem, the beloved seems to offer both a new *physical* home and, personally, the security and support that a home should embody. And yet the structuring of the rhetoric, with its opening conditional 'If' and its repeated questioning throughout, still gestures towards underlying anxieties concerning the possibility of this desire coming to fruition. Indeed, whilst the sequence as a whole moves to the assertion of a vast, expansive, all-encompassing love (Sonnet 43: see discussion in Chapter 1), EBB's poems on human love overall constantly reveal how difficult a meaningful relationship and secure home are to attain in reality, since her speakers and protagonists are repeatedly betrayed, manipulated and even annihilated. Moreover, as I explore in the following chapter, this search for a meaningful emotional relationship and a secure and supportive home becomes even more fraught when viewed within wider political and national contexts.

4

The Search for a Political Home

In the last chapter I explored some of the ways in which the speakers and protagonists of EBB's poems of the 1830s and 1840s seek for the security of a 'home' through human relationships and love, and how this search is often defeated by dominant gender expectations, brutal power relations and patterns of betrayal. For whilst EBB's body of poetry repeatedly exposes the tensions which lie at the heart of emotional and sexual relationships, it is rarely able to offer a workable solution to them. The women in the ballads, for example, are constantly pushed to despair and self-annihilation, and the positive egalitarian world depicted in 'An Island' remains illusory and an imaginative fabrication. Even with 'Lady Geraldine's Court-ship' and the highly-personal *Sonnets from the Portuguese*, in which the right to speech and equality is asserted, the establishment of a meaningful relationship remains highly problematic, founded upon a series of complex negotiations and the consideration of anxieties and concerns which might, at least in part, remain unresolved.

In this chapter I explore a different notion of 'home' in EBB's work, that of the free, liberal and supportive nation state which emerges from EBB's lifelong obsession with politics. As I noted in Chapter 1, and as I have explored in detail elsewhere,[1] EBB was fascinated by politics from an early age, influenced by the male members of her family – her father, her Uncle Samuel and her brother, Edward – all of whom were active participants in the Whig party. As the party of opposition throughout the final decades of the eighteenth century and the early decades of the nineteenth, the Whigs had at the heart of their political philosophy a commitment to protecting the legal, civil and religious rights of the individual, rights for which EBB would spend much of her poetic career fighting. Indeed, the young EBB was already taking a public stance on these issues as early as 1817 when, aged just eleven, she sent a letter to the Lord Lieutenant of Herefordshire, Lord Somers, condemning the (temporary) suspension of the Habeas Corpus, one of the cornerstones of individual liberty, by Liverpool's Tory government. Writing in a passionate and informed manner, EBB defines the Habeas Corpus as 'that sacred star which is now pillaged of its rays to satisfy the interests of the Ministers' (*Correspondence* 1:42) before tracing its history back to King John and arguing that, although the people of past ages might have laboured under intense hardship, they at least had the knowledge that they were free. That assurance, she suggests, is no longer available and so she calls on the people to 'despise our Tyrants' and to remain, as she signs the letter, 'The Friend of liberty' (*Correspondence* 1:42–3).

Although EBB was not yet in her teens when she wrote this letter, it raises a fundamental concern with the relations between individual liberty and the nation state which would occupy her, in one form or another, for the rest of her life. For EBB's career spans five decades which witnessed a series of major nationalist uprisings across Europe as country after country, galvanized by the ideals of the French Revolution, rose up to claim independence, throw off occupying forces, and achieve unification. As a politically-driven poet, this nationalist drive fascinated EBB and became the basis of many of her most interesting works. Indeed, as I noted in Chapter 1, EBB's career as a published poet began with a specific focus on the issues surrounding the Greek national state. Her early epic, *The Battle of Marathon*, for example, celebrates the legendary defeat of the invading Persians by a vastly-outnumbered Greek army in 490BC, and can clearly be related to early-nineteenth-century debates surrounding Greece's long-standing occupation by the Turks. Then, in her first properly published poems of the early 1820s, EBB dealt explicitly with the Greek War of Independence which had broken out in 1821, celebrating Greece as 'the Parent of the free' ('Thoughts awakened by contemplating a piece of the palm', l.18) and championing Byron's part in the conflict in both 'Stanzas on the Death of Lord Byron' and *An Essay on Mind*. As she would write to Hugh Stuart Boyd in 1828, her support for the Greek cause would never waver since '[t]he Greeks are Greeks by name & soil & descent' and she 'would not have tyrants breathe where poets sang,—or slaves tread in the footsteps of heroes!' (*Correspondence* 2:108–9).

This concern with Greek nationalism is further evidenced in another poem in the *Essay on Mind* collection, the critically-neglected 'Riga's Last Song'. Structured in the form of a monologue, this poem is spoken by one of the earliest heroes of the Greek cause, Rhigas Feraios (1757–98), a champion of republicanism who wrote political pamphlets, poetry and histories of Greece calling for political uprising and foregrounding the stark disparity between the country's heroic past and its current plight under Ottoman rule. In 1797, however, whilst on his way to revolutionize the Balkans, Rhigas was captured at Trieste by the Austrians and given over to the Turks for execution, the focus of EBB's poem. Here, the 'last song' of Riga (the spelling is an established alternative) focuses on Greece's imposing landscape and sites of past military successes – Souli, Marathon, Thermopylæ – before calling on the people, '[t]he dark Greek pride crouched in their eye' (l.26), to rise up and regain the liberty of the country. As Riga asserts, '[t]hough the dust be fettered, the spirit is free' and he therefore seeks to leave behind him '[t]he stirrings of Freedom's mighty mind' (ll.11; 14). Although the poem ends with a coda in which an omniscient narrative voice records the severing of Riga's head, the final emphasis, recalling the close of the elegy to Byron, is on his 'mute lyre' (l.38) which will paradoxically continue to sound from the grave through his inspirational writings.

Riga's martyrdom made him a powerful symbol of resistance for the Greeks and the placing of the poem in this volume foregrounds again the figure of the political hero which was coming to fascinate EBB. Indeed, this concern is further established in another political poem of the 1826 volume, 'On a Picture of Riego's Widow', which, in its celebration of Spanish revolutionaries, draws upon EBB's understanding of the push for nationalist self-determination in the Latin countries in the early 1820s. The name in the title refers to Rafael del Riego y Núñez (1784–1823), the leader of the movement that temporarily secured the restoration of the Cortes constitution in 1820 but who was later executed as a traitor by French forces seeking to re-establish reactionary control. (The popular Spanish revolutionary song, *Himno de Riego*, which became the national anthem under the republic, was named after him.) But the chief focus of the poem is rather his wife, Teresa del Riego, whose picture the speaker admires for its depiction of the calm face of the 'Daughter of Spain' (l.1), evidencing strength and commitment to the revolutionary cause even whilst in anguish at her husband's death: 'We look upon the Widow's face,/ And only read the Patriot's woe!' (ll.7–8). As Dorothy Mermin notes, Riego's widow 'shows her defiance of tyranny not by proclaiming her feelings but by concealing them.'[2] Significantly, however, EBB shifts the emphasis at the end of the poem to condemnation of the *British* government for their rejection of Teresa's request for intervention to save Riego, a key concern throughout her work. Consequently, the poem suggests, the portrait is likely to produce feelings of shame in British viewers since 'if British souls they bear,/ 'Twill start the crimson in the cheek/ To see Riego's widow THERE!' (ll.38–40).

Interestingly, EBB did not leave her treatment of Riego's widow here but returned to it in 'The Death-Bed of Teresa Del Riego', a poem she included in her 1833 volume. Focusing on Teresa's dead body in a way which almost fetishises it (her hair in particular is viewed as a form of relic), this poem laments the death of the political exile removed from her native Spain by constructing her as 'Beautiful form of woman' (l.13), a pertinent combination of politics and femininity. Throughout her career, EBB would remain fascinated by the figure of the female revolutionary and woman's relation to nationalist politics (as witnessed, for example, in *Aurora Leigh* and 'Mother and Poet': see Chapter 5 and Conclusion) and she would repeatedly foreground the importance of women in the process of establishing a supportive nation state. Certainly, hers was a politics where issues of gender were always crucial.

This relation between nationalist politics and the failure to establish a secure political home for the state's citizens is explored in more detail in a rarely-examined work included in *Poems* (1844), the fascinating 'Crowned and Buried'. Again, this poem is a form of elegy which deploys the return of Napoleon's ashes from St Helena for repatriation and internment in the Hotel des Invalides in Paris as a means of articulating EBB's ambiguous feelings about the great leader's career and his relation to the nationalist ideals of the French Revolution. For here EBB almost appears to hero-worship Napoleon for his astonishing rise to power and his overthrowing of corrupt European monarchs, emphasizing the power of his name – that signifier of heroism in many of her political poems – to engender both adoration and fear: '[t]he world's face changed to hear it' (l.31). Indeed, the early stanzas of the poem construct Napoleon through images of the sublime (he is compared to 'lightning.../ Scathing the cedars of the world' and his name is a 'trumpet' reminiscent of the apocalypse, ll.4–5; 9), therefore almost making him into a Titan figure. Interestingly, this model of Napoleon was one which EBB also promoted in her correspondence to Mary Russell Mitford in 1844, where she argued that 'Napoleon was cast in the heroic mould, & fell naturally into the heroic gesture...He [was] as statuesque as Hercules, though in boots!' (*Mitford* 2:454). And yet despite this, 'Crowned and Buried' also asserts how Napoleon's autocratic and tyrannous quest to redraw European boundaries 'afresh in blood' (l.40) effectively sold the French people out by prioritizing personal gain over the fundamental revolutionary ideals of liberty, fraternity and equality:

> For, verily, though France augustly rose
> With that raised NAME, and did assume by such
> The purple of the world, none gave so much
> As she, in purchase – to speak plain, in loss –
> Whose hand, toward freedom stretched, dropped paralysed...
>
> (ll.49–53)

As Roy Gridley notes, the poem appears to 'scorn the transformation of the Republic into Empire',[3] and yet EBB remains ambivalent about Napoleon's legacy, acknowledging his position as 'despot' (l.147) but ultimately seeming unable to pass judgement: 'I think this grave stronger than thrones. But whether/ The crowned Napoleon or the buried clay/ Be worthier, I discern not. Angels may' (ll.166–8). As I argue in Chapter 5, however, EBB's continued interest in French politics, her admiration of great French writers like George Sand, Honoré de Balzac and Eugène Sue, and her frequent residencies in Paris following her move to the Continent, meant that she would come to view France decisively as the country which had the most potential for transformative socio-political and aesthetic experience – a view, I suggest, that she puts at the very heart of *Aurora Leigh* with its celebration of France as '[t]his poet of the nations' (*Aurora Leigh*, 6:54).

When ordering *Poems* (1844), EBB placed 'Crowned and Buried' next to 'Crowned and Wedded', her most interesting poem on Victoria which promotes the young queen as a model of benevolent, 'feminized' leadership in contrast to Napoleon's masculinist autocracy. Yet the volume overall is highly critical of the British nation state and particularly the impact of its status as the first industrialized nation. In 'The Cry of the Human', for example, EBB reflects, in true Carlylean mode, on '[t]he curse of gold upon the land' (l.46) which prioritizes profit and the cash nexus over humanitarian concerns and morality, thereby intensifying the already stark disparity between the classes: 'The rich preach "rights" and future days,/ And hear no angel scoffing, – / The poor die mute – with starving gaze' (ll.50–2). And it is this emphasis on alienation and exploitation which is then located at the very centre of that far more famous poem which is seemingly connected to 'The Cry of the Human' through its title, 'The Cry of the Children'.

As EBB notes in her correspondence, the initial inspiration for 'The Cry of the Children' was her reading of the 1843 *Report of the Royal Commission on the Employment of Children and Very Young People in Mines and Factories*, a government paper written partly by her friend Richard Hengist Horne which recorded the vast range of social problems engendered by industrialization. Indeed, the report had such an impact on EBB, she told Boyd, that the first stanza of her poetic response 'came into my head in a hurricane' (*Correspondence* 7:331). The result is a thirteen-stanza work which, despite its heavy emotional burden and sometimes stylized depiction of the children and their working environments, is a highly-significant poem in EBB's *oeuvre* and one which, in Helen Cooper's phrasing, is 'powerful...technically and politically.'[4] For in its pointed address to 'my brothers' (the phrasing is repeated three times in the first two stanzas, indicating that it is the men in power who EBB seeks to persuade), the poem condemns a society which has transformed its children into weary, exhausted figures who are alienated from both youth and joy in nature and consequently left envying Little Alice who is 'lulled and still' in the grave (l.49). Indeed, these opening stanzas function to emphasize the idea that industrialization even breaks down the fundamental mother-child bond at the heart of the family unit, for the mothers here are incapable of offering any relief when their offspring are '[w]eeping sore before the[ir] bosoms' (l.23). For a poet who repeatedly used mothering and the breast as images of nurturing and potential socio-political development (for example, in *Aurora Leigh*), this depiction is horrific and far removed from the benevolent security associated with the family unit in a poem like Felicia Hemans' 'Homes of England' (1827). The female influence which EBB repeatedly suggests is essential for the effective running of the nation is therefore eradicated here in what the speaker ironically terms 'the country of the free' and 'our happy Fatherland' (ll.12; 24).

This 'Fatherland', with its significant linking of brutal industrial processes and the brutality of hegemonic masculinity, is everywhere felt in the poem as the children emphasize their entrapment in a system which mechanizes their whole world:

> 'For, all day, the wheels are droning, turning, –
>   Their wind comes in our faces, –
> Till our hearts turn, – our heads, with pulses burning,
>   And the walls turn in their places.
> Turns the sky in the high window blank and reeling,
>   Turns the long light that drops adown the wall,
> Turn the black flies that crawl along the ceiling,
>   All are turning, all the day, and we with all.
> And all day, the iron wheels are droning,
>   And sometimes we could pray,
> "O ye wheels," (breaking out in a mad moaning)
>   'Stop! be silent for to-day."'

(ll.77–88)

With its striking use of repetitions and present participles, this stanza articulates a Dantesque circle of hell where the wind of nature is replaced by the rush of air created by the machinery's movement and where spatial relations, in a manner pushing towards gothic, become so distorted that '[a]ll are turning...and we with all.' Equally significant is the children's sole pleading 'prayer' for the wheels to be silent, for as the following four

61

stanzas reveal, the machinery affects the children to such an extent that their souls too '[s]pin on blindly in the dark' (l.100) and consequently they can only conceive of God as the type of their master who 'commands us to work on' (ll.128). Indeed, in believing that God is 'speechless as stone' (l.126) and therefore uncritical of the system which exploits them, the children are exiled from yet another source of support and hope and denied the knowledge that 'this cold metallic motion/ Is not all the life God fashions or reveals' (ll.93-4). Rather, as Angela Leighton emphasizes, the children envisage heaven as merely another element of that overarching 'barbaric and brutal Symbolic Order' underpinning the world of the poem, a situation which aligns them in part with that array of speakers and protagonists exiled from a spiritual home with God which I considered in Chapter 2.[5]

It is in the final shocking stanza, however, that traditional religion is most clearly subverted as EBB draws the reader into a seemingly innocent comparison between the children and angels addressing the deity, only then to have them deliver a damning curse in the style of an Old Testament prophet:

> 'How long,' they say, 'how long, O cruel nation,
>   Will you stand, to move the world, on a child's heart, –
> Stifle down with a mailed heel its palpitation,
>   And tread onward to your throne amid the mark?
> Our blood splashes upward, O gold-heaper,
>   And your purple shows your path!
> But the child's sob in the silence curses deeper
>   Than the strong man in his wrath.'

(ll.153-60)

With its fierce condemnation of a nation which symbolically treads on the bodies and hearts of those children it requires to support its capitalist structures – imagery of the broken body that will become increasingly central to EBB's political writings – this stanza is a stunning close to a poem which exposes the horrors of the early-Victorian industrial system and which ridicules the idea that Britain offers a supportive, secure 'home' to its people. Both weeping and cursing are deployed as political acts in this poem and both, EBB appears to argue, are necessary in order to raise awareness and bring about social transformation.[6] Rather than wallowing in sentimentality, then, as some critics have suggested, this poem is highly effective in its political message and a central work in EBB's ongoing exploration of nationalist politics. Indeed, it is possibly as a result of reading this particular poem that the great Victorian sage, Thomas Carlyle, wrote to EBB suggesting that a thinker of her 'insight and veracity' should turn to writing prose in these 'days of crisis' (*Correspondence* 9:122). EBB, however, was always firm in her belief that *poetry* offered the most effective means of exposing political truths and the 'evil' which is 'in the system' (*Correspondence* 11:43). Certainly, it was this system and the often brutal relations it established between the individual and the state which she was to interrogate in even more confrontational manner in her bold attack on *American* politics, 'The Runaway Slave at Pilgrim's Point'.

As many critics have pointed out, 'The Runaway Slave at Pilgrim's Point' was the first poem which EBB completed after she herself ran away from the tyranny of her father by marrying Robert. Moreover, the poem can be read, at least in part, as a repudiation of EBB's own family background given that, until the early 1830s, a major constituent of the Barrett family money was derived from sugar produced on slave plantations in Jamaica.[7] As Alan Richardson argues in his consideration of slavery in the early nineteenth century, '[a]t a time when sugaring one's tea carried political and moral overtones, few could remain unaware of one of the burning contradictions of British ideology.... The same nation that prided itself on individual liberties was the major European trafficker in human flesh, with a colonial system increasingly dependent on slave labour.'[8] Although trafficking was banned in 1807, this resulted in many plantations relying on breeding slaves for labour. The Barrett family's commitment to slavery therefore sits particularly uncomfortably with their commitment to the Whig concerns with the legal, civil and religious rights of the individual. Indeed, when the industry collapsed in the early 1830s following uprisings on the plantations, declining sugar prices, and the eventual abolition of slavery in the colonies, EBB commented to her friend Julia Martin that, despite being faced with the loss of Hope End (the home was sold and the family moved first to Sidmouth and then to London), she was 'glad, and always shall be, that the negroes are – virtually – free!'

(*Correspondence* 3:86).

This is an intriguing context for 'The Runaway Slave', although its more pressing context is obviously the contemporary debates about slavery in America in the 1840s, debates which would eventually lead to the outbreak of the Civil War in 1861. For in 1845, following the success of *Poems*, EBB was invited by the Boston anti-slavery annual, *The Liberty Bell*, to submit a poem to help raise money for the abolitionist cause ('The Runaway Slave' eventually appeared in the 1848 annual, published in December 1847). As Marjorie Stone has detailed, *The Liberty Bell* featured works by many major abolitionists of the period, including William Lloyd Garrison, Frederick Douglass, Theodore Parker, Elizabeth Pease and Harriet Martineau, so EBB was in strong company.[9] But this did not stop her having concerns about the poem she produced, telling Mary Russell Mitford that she 'could not help making it bitter' (*Mitford* 3:203) and expressing her fear to Hugh Stuart Boyd that it was 'too ferocious, perhaps, for the Americans to publish' (*Correspondence* 14:86). Indeed, in what became her key dramatic monologue, spoken by a female slave who is raped by a group of slave owners, murders her child, and then runs away to Pilgrim's Point to condemn the dominant political system of America, EBB powerfully engages with a complex nexus of issues concerning race, gender, sexuality and nation. It is highly significant, therefore, that when EBB reprinted the work in *Poems* (1850), she placed it next to 'The Cry of the Children', for both poems focus specifically on the ways in which nations – America and Britain respectively – alienate whole groups from their socio-political structures rather than seeking to accommodate and support them in a secure political home. Whilst EBB suggested to Mitford that she arranged this ordering to 'appear impartial as to national grievances' (*Mitford* 3:310), the effect is rather to foreground even further her concerns with nationalist politics and her belief, as she would phrase it in *Casa Guidi Windows*, that 'great nations have great shames' (Part 2, l.648).

As Julia Markus has noted, the original version of 'The Runaway Slave' was entitled 'Mad and Black at Pilgrim's Point'.[10] Throughout the majority of the poem, however, the slave's arguments come across as focused, well-reasoned and astute, with a line of thinking which, although often shocking, almost always remains logical. Indeed, as she explicitly states, 'I am not mad: I am black' (l.218), a phrasing which pinpoints the impact of racist ideology as the cause of her actions rather than any innate psychological instability. Certainly the poem opens confidently with the speaker asserting her subject position through the repeated 'I' structure at the start of four of the seven lines of the first stanza, an affirmative stance which, as Helen Cooper suggests, marks a distinct shift from the more hesitant voice of the earlier ballads and clearly points towards that strength of expression found in *Casa Guidi Windows* and *Aurora Leigh*.[11] Further, this notion of strength is reiterated by the first verb of the poem: 'stand'. For the speaker, although triply disenfranchised by dominant society (as black, female and a slave), boldly asserts her right to return to the place of the Pilgrim Fathers' arrival, to invoke their spirits, and to expose their legacy. Indeed, in a manner which prefigures the implicit arguments regarding America's inherent history of violence which can be found in Sylvia Plath's stunning poem, 'Cut' (*Ariel*, 1965), EBB's slave makes explicit and ironic connections between the pilgrims who arrived in America seeking sanctuary from persecution and their slave-owning descendants who now 'in your names' work 'sin and woe' (l.14).

This reinterpretation of history in order to expose the oppressive structures of power and exploitation at the centre of the American nation is fundamental to the poem as the slave kneels where the pilgrim father kneeled, not to confirm their blessing of 'freedoms evermore' (1.21) but to narrate an alternative national story of brutality which will subsequently 'curse this land' (1.20). Interestingly, this kneeling posture offers a potential subversion of that major icon of abolition produced by Josiah Wedgwood in 1787 in which a slave in chains is depicted on one bent knee, his hands clasped in front of him in pleading manner whilst he asks 'Am I Not a Man and a Brother?'[12] In contrast, there is no pleading by EBB's female slave but rational argument and condemnation, which is witnessed initially in her exploration of the fragile premises of the colour system upon which slavery is based. For as she argues, whilst many black things in nature are celebrated (birds, streams, frogs, the night), the blackness of the slaves' skin 'shuts like prison bars' (1.39). These distinctions serve to highlight, as

65

the poem emphasizes throughout, the artificiality of the white/
black binary at the heart of racist ideology and a fundamentally
social construction which is employed to 'justify' horrific
systems of physical, psychological and sexual abuse.

This abuse is foregrounded uncompromisingly in the second
part of the poem (stanzas VII–XXVIII) where the shift into the
past tense enables the slave to recount those experiences which
have led to her present situation. Opening with the line 'I am
black, I am black' (l.57), a statement which is repeated
throughout as a forceful assertion of her subject position, the
speaker recalls her relationship with another slave, conducted
covertly through whispers and singing, which enabled them to
transcend the system that robbed them of their identity, liberty
and dignity: 'our spirits grew/ As free as if unsold, unbought'
(ll.64–5). Indeed, the image of the lover carving the speaker 'a
bowl of the cocoa-nut/ Through the roar of the hurricanes' (ll.76–
7) functions as a symbolic indicator of the peace he offers her
even whilst they are being degraded by the drivers and slave
master. And yet this mode of resistance is quickly dissolved by
the system it seeks to challenge as the lover is taken away and
murdered, his 'blood's mark' left 'in the dust' (l.97) as a signifier
of the brutal power structures at the heart of slavery. This is only
the first of several key instances of violence conducted against
the body, however, where, in an important prefiguring of the
politics of *Aurora Leigh*, bodies are beaten, broken, marked, and,
in the case of the slave herself, gang-raped by the representa-
tives of the state and power:

> Wrong, followed by a deeper wrong!
>   Mere grief's too good for such as I.
> So the white men brought the shame ere long
>   To strangle the sob of my agony.
> They would not leave me for my dull
> Wet eyes! – it was too merciful
>   To let me weep pure tears and die.

(ll.99–105)

As Marjorie Stone has noted in her study of the manuscript of
this poem in Wellesley College Library, EBB originally con-
ceived the slave as male.[13] By switching the gender, then, EBB
was able to heighten both the depiction of abuse and the slave's
subjection to white male systems of violence. For despite the

inexplicit reference to rape here, the outcome is blatantly evident when, in the next stanza, the slave reports 'I wore a child upon my breast' (l.107). Moreover, in keeping with the power differentials embedded in the white/black, male/female dichotomies running throughout the poem, the horror of the violation is intensified further by the fact that the child is both male and white, and, as the speaker highlights, 'far too white... too white for me' (l.116). To the slave, the child already seems to exhibit the look of 'the master-right' (l.126), and consequently, in one of the most disturbing scenes in EBB's work overall, she smothers him in his shawl until he lies dead in her arms, 'a stiffening cold' (l.152). The drawn-out description of this process, which takes up five stanzas (XVIII–XXII), is told in a chillingly calm manner, similar to the recounting of the killing of Porphyria by the male speaker in Robert Browning's poem 'Porphyria's Lover' (published 1842). But as Helen Cooper argues, the act of infanticide here has a peculiar logic to it 'in a culture that violently distorts the bond between mother and child.'[14] As with 'The Cry of the Children', then, the impact of systems of exploitation serves to damage the maternal bond in a way which firmly undermines the hope of bringing a supportive nation state into being. Indeed, only by burying her white child in the black earth – an act which signals, as Deirdre David argues, a reversal of the power politics at the heart of the master/slave relationship[15] – can the slave and her child achieve any degree of reconciliation.

In another parallel with 'The Cry of the Children', 'The Runaway Slave' also overtly questions the place of religion in upholding, even promoting, a system which disenfranchises and degrades whole sectors of society. For the slave is fundamentally unable to relate to a God who would 'cast his work away/ Under the feet of his white creatures' (ll.25–6) and questions why, when her lover is killed, God sits '[c]old-ly... behind the sun' and 'wilt not speak' (ll.89; 91) – a phrasing which clearly recalls the God who is 'speechless as stone' in 'The Cry of the Children'. Indeed, in the horrifying depiction of God's 'white angels' sucking out the soul of her child (ll.155–61), an image which shockingly relocates the act of murder to heaven itself, there is a strong suggestion that established religion is as potentially violent as many aspects of the slave system and that God, as Linda M. Lewis argues, is again 'merely master among masters.'[16]

With the return to the site of Pilgrim's Point in the final part of the poem, however, the power which the slave found in the act of infanticide is augmented further as she confronts the group of 'hunter sons' (1.204) surrounding her in the final tragic scene. And it is here that the slave's rhetoric gets to the very heart of those debates concerning the relations between the individual and the nation state which EBB has been exploring for the past two decades. For before she commits suicide from the rock where the Pilgrim fathers landed, in what David terms 'a dreadful parody of the liberation achieved by [the] white pilgrims',[17] the slave faces 'the Washington-race' head on and exposes the concept of 'free America' as nothing more than a myth (11.221-2). Indeed, the black eagle, the traditional symbol of American democracy, is, in the slave's words, 'killed...at nest' (1.208), an image which gestures toward the notion of the destroyed home running through EBB's work and which also specifically recalls the violated swan's nest in EBB's earlier ballad (see Chapter 3). As the poem emphasizes, therefore, America already is, and arguably always has been, that house divided against itself which Abraham Lincoln would famously term it a decade later.[18] Consequently, in a powerful gesture of defiance against the '[w]hips' and 'curses' of America (1.232), the speaker calls on all slaves to rise up and liberate themselves: 'From these sands/ Up to the mountains, lift your hands,/ O slaves, and end what I begun!' (11.229–31). Only then might a nation state be born that offers hope and security for all its citizens.

'The Runaway Slave at Pilgrim's Point' is one of EBB's most astonishing works, composed on an issue which crystallized her key concerns with oppression, the nation and gender. Indeed, as Angela Leighton rightly points out, '[t]his is a poem which is almost entirely free of sentimentality because, for all its emotional rhetoric, it holds nothing sacred. Democracy, religious liberty, family ancestry and even mother love cannot be kept ..."unstain'd".'[19] EBB would return to the issue of slavery in two later poems, 'Hiram Powers "Greek Slave"' and 'A Curse for a Nation', but following her move to Europe the key political focus for the remainder of her career became Italy's push for freedom from Austrian control and the achievement of complete unification. A full discussion of *Casa Guidi Windows*, EBB's major poem on the Italian situation, is beyond the scope of this chapter and I have discussed it in detail elsewhere,[20] but as I explored in Chapter 1, it saw EBB calling for a new kind of poetics which would galvanize military and religious leaders and marshal the strength of 'Il popolo' in order to 'make of Italy a nation' (Part 1, ll.499; 840). Although the 1848–9 revolutions which the poem maps out ultimately failed, EBB's commitment to Italian unification did not. Indeed, as she powerfully puts it in Part Two of the poem, 'Ye stamp no nation out, though day and night/ Ye tread them with that absolute heel which grates/ And grinds them flat' (Part 2, ll.337–9). Significantly, at the close of *Casa Guidi Windows*, EBB returns to that notion of 'mothering' which had been present in several of her previous political poems as she depicts her own son, Penini, standing at the window of their apartment:

> The sun strikes, through my windows, up the floor;
> Stand out in it, my own young Florentine,
> Not two years old, and let me see thee more!
> It grows along thy amber curls, to shine
> Brighter than elsewhere.

> (2:742–6)

As I have suggested previously, this image both draws upon the trope of the classical epic hero which EBB deployed in her early work, *The Battle of Marathon*, and replaces that earlier inspirational figure of the young boy singing 'O bella libertà, O bella!' beneath the apartment window (1:3) as the symbol of a new future.[21] Indeed, Penini is constructed here as nothing less than 'my blue-eyed prophet' (2:757) who offers reassurance that unification and political freedom may eventually be possible. In sharp contrast to the depictions of distorted mothering and broken maternal bonds found in works like 'The Cry of the Children' and 'The Runaway Slave', then, *Casa Guidi Windows* closes with the emphasis on the need for supportive and nurturing motherhood if a secure political state is ever to be achieved.[22]

Whilst EBB's engagement with the Italian *Risorgimento* constitutes her most sustained treatment of nationalist politics, it evidently develops out of, and builds upon, that interest in nationalism and the relations between the individual and the state which she had been exploring in both her poetry and her private correspondence since her early teens. Indeed, whether she was writing about the need for a country's liberation and unification, as with her work on Greece, Spain and Italy, or whether she was writing about the need for a country to tackle structures which exploit and disenfranchise particular groups, as in 'The Cry of the Children' and 'The Runaway Slave at Pilgrim's Point', the notion of a supportive state was fundamental to the ideal of home she constantly interrogated in her work, even if it often seemed impossible to bring into being. It was with her next major work, however, the ground-breaking *Aurora Leigh*, that EBB came nearest to envisaging how a secure and supportive home might actually be attained.

5

Restructuring Home:
Aurora Leigh

In the last three chapters I have explored how the speakers and protagonists of EBB's poems are often depicted searching for a home which is variously associated with spiritual security, a meaningful emotional relationship, or the establishment of an inclusive and politically-liberal nation state. Time and again, however, this nominal home remains finally unattainable, as at-oneness with Christ or God is deferred or unfulfilled, love and sexual relations are found to be grounded in problematic and often brutal power games, and dominant political structures repeatedly fail the individual, social group or even whole country. Nevertheless, or maybe because of this, the process of the search itself is one which EBB's poetic speakers constantly and insistently rehearse.

In this chapter, I examine a text, the intellectually intriguing and formally innovative *Aurora Leigh*, where the attainment of home *is* finally achieved. For the long narrative structure of *Aurora Leigh*, which is principally founded upon a series of crucial journeys (from Italy to England, England to France, and France to Italy), eventually enables the eponymous heroine to find a resolution to the quest for home which draws together and interweaves the spiritual, the emotional and the political, along with other important elements. As I suggest in the Conclusion to this book, however, this achievement of a more holistic home is only temporary since EBB's subsequent work, in *Poems Before Congress* (1860) and the posthumous *Last Poems* (1862), witnesses fragmentation replacing unity once again. Nevertheless, *Aurora Leigh* is crucial for its detailed and wide-

71

ranging exploration of what a meaningful home might be and how it might be structured.

Aurora Leigh is an extraordinary poem by any standards and took EBB over a decade to bring to fruition. Indeed, as early as 1841, EBB was seeking advice from Mary Russell Mitford on a suitable subject for the longer poem she wished to write. Mitford's suggestion was Napoleon, a figure EBB had tackled in 'Crowned and Buried', but at this stage EBB replied that she was rather drawn to a female subject, Joan of Arc. 'I do not think with you that an objection to a military-glory-subject reverberates necessarily against Joan,' she speculated; 'If I wrote of her, it wd. not be of "a great general" but of a great enthusiast... preserving faithfully & tenderly her womanly nature unrusted in the iron which sheathes it' (*Correspondence* 5:173). This, then, is the initial prototype for the protagonist of EBB's planned poem (as it might also have been for 'The Romaunt of the Page'), a female figure who demonstrates those characteristics of strength, resolve and political drive which Aurora would come to embody. Four years later, however, EBB had decided against an historical subject and sought instead to create a new poem in the vein of 'Lady Geraldine's Courtship', the poem which had consolidated her commitment to an overt focus on contemporary socio-political issues. As EBB wrote to her future husband in a now-famous letter of February 1845:

> my chief *intention* just now is the writing of a sort of novel-poem – a poem as completely modern as 'Geraldine's Courtship,' running into the midst of our conventions, & rushing into drawingrooms & the like 'where angels fear to tread'; – & so, meeting face to face & without mask, the Humanity of the age, & speaking the truth as I conceive of it, out plainly. (*Correspondence* 10:102–3)

Modern, defying conventions, taking risks, and voicing 'plainly' that which society would rather not hear: such a poem, Robert responded enthusiastically, would be a 'fearless fresh living work' and 'the *only* Poem to be undertaken now by you or anyone that *is* a Poet at all' (*Correspondence* 10:118).

Certainly *Aurora Leigh* would be EBB's most extensive and discursive treatment of the contemporary world to date. For intertwined with the narrative of Aurora's development as a successful woman poet – the focus which makes the poem into a proto-feminist version of the *künstlerroman* that EBB had first found in Beattie's *The Minstrel* and which had been treated more recently in Wordsworth's *The Prelude* (1850) – is an impressive interrogation of issues as varied as the Condition of England, socialism, utilitarianism, the 'woman question', prostitution, education, the role of religion, the role of work, life in the new urban environments, spiritualism, and many other concerns and events which form part of what Aurora terms 'this live, throbbing age' (*Aurora Leigh* 5:203). As Marjorie Stone points out in her important study of the poem, '[t]opical references jostle on every page.'[1] Moreover, as I noted in Chapter 1, EBB was aware that such a politically-engaged and complex work required a new structure and form, the 'novel-poem' as she termed it in her 1845 letter to Robert. In part, this generically-mixed form saw EBB returning to the epic conventions which she had first engaged with in *The Battle of Marathon* three decades earlier, and yet *Aurora Leigh* effectively subverts both classical epic's standard form and content. For rather than the traditional twelve-book structure which focuses on a male warrior who undertakes a series of arduous tasks in order to establish a nation, EBB's poem employs a nine-book structure and focuses on a contemporary woman poet who undertakes a series of arduous tasks in order to establish her professional identity and construct a new socio-political order with the help of a redeemed 'fallen woman' and a reformed socialist-philanthropist. Consequently, as Susan Stanford Friedman argues, 'the heroic [is] redefined in female terms [and] the personal made public.'[2] EBB then combines this reconfiguration of the epic with some of the key techniques which she had appropriated from the British and European realist fiction that she so avidly read, including character growth and development, interweaved narrative arcs, and the use of dialogue and conversation as a means of debating ideas. For as she wrote to Mitford in 1844:

> where is the obstacle to making as interesting a story of a poem as of a prose work?...Conversations & events, why may they not be given as rapidly & passionately & lucidly in verse as in prose...I want to write a poem of a new class, in a measure...having unity, as a work of art, – & admitting of as much philosophical dreaming & digression (which is in fact a characteristic of the age) as I like to use.

Might it not be done, even if I could not do it? & I think of trying at any rate. (*Correspondence* 9:304)

Without doubt, the poem is 'of a new class' and often a radical one at that. Indeed, as Mary Sanders Pollock has noted, the result of EBB's greatest formal experiment is 'a polyphonic work of many layers, voices, and genres' which 'weaves' together autobiographical narrative, reported and spoken life stories, lyrical passages, detailed description, socio-political commentary, and theoretical speculation about life and art.[3] In its eleven thousand lines of blank verse (making it, one reviewer complained, longer than Milton's *Paradise Lost*[4]), EBB threw with full force her greatest challenge to the literary, cultural and social establishment of her day so that the poem, to borrow a phrase from Emily Dickinson, the great American poet who hero-worshipped EBB, 'dances like a Bomb, abroad'.[5] Certainly, as EBB herself indicates in the poem's dedication to John Kenyon, *Aurora Leigh* constitutes what she considered 'the most mature of my works, and the one into which my highest convictions upon Life and Art have entered.' As I argue in this chapter, it is particularly through Aurora's progression, personal and professional, that these 'convictions' are worked out, as Aurora acquires strategies for resisting limited thinking and systematic oppression and thereby creates possibilities for both socio-political change and the construction of that secure and meaningful home which, I have suggested, becomes increasingly central to EBB's poetics.

Much of Aurora's quest for this eventual home, like that of many of the poetic speakers I examined in Chapter 3, is bound up with her negotiation of the dominant nineteenth-century family unit. As Dorothy Mermin has detailed,[6] this begins early for Aurora when she is '[u]nmothered' (1:95) at four years old and subsequently raised by her English father in the beautiful Tuscan landscape, '[a]mong the mountains above Pelago' (1:111). It is here, in an environment where nurturing nature takes over from Aurora's dead Italian mother, that resistance to dominant systems of thought begins, not only for Aurora but for her father as well. In renouncing his utilitarian concerns with Da Vinci's drainage system (1:72), a renunciation of the kind Romney will later need to make, Aurora's father becomes increasingly inspired by the romantic associations of the Italian countryside and consequently seeks to 'throw off the old conventions' (1:177) whilst encouraging his daughter to interrogate and challenge inflexible systems of thought:

> He sent the schools to school, demonstrating
> A fool will pass for such through one mistake,
> While a philosopher will pass for such,
> Through said mistakes being ventured in the gross
> And heaped up to a system.

(1:194–8)

It is this challenge to received ideas and dominant belief systems, an issue which EBB had first tackled in *An Essay on Mind*, which is central to the arguments of *Aurora Leigh* overall and which, for both Aurora and, later, Marian, is interlinked with, and to large degree dependent upon, the reconfiguration of traditional feminine roles. Indeed, the much critically-debated scene where Aurora gazes at the picture of her dead mother as it fragments and reproduces itself into iconic portrayals of various female types – angel, witch, muse, Psyche, the Virgin Mary, Lamia, Medusa (1:128-73) – is the earliest reference to the need to reject such inherited models, just as the speaker at the opening of *Casa Guidi Windows* argues for the need to reject the disabling feminine images of Italy in order to bring about political change.[7] As Aurora subsequently develops, what her mother represents becomes both a source of loss, engendering 'a mother-want about the world' (1:40), and something to be feared as she seeks to define herself *against* such stereotypical feminine subject positions and the oppressive socializing systems they embody. Indeed, as Helen Cooper has argued, the older Aurora, reflecting back on this youthful experience, clearly recognizes 'that woman's identity is created by the cultural economy', an economy which works hard to reinforce mythic constructs rather than suggesting the possibility of art as vocation.[8]

The greatest danger of succumbing to these socializing systems and dominant cultural types, however, comes not in Italy but in England, when, following the death of her father, Aurora is forcibly removed from her home country and thrust on the first of those journeys which are structurally central to the text:

Ten nights and days we voyaged on the deep;
Ten nights and days without the common face
Of any day or night; the moon and sun
Cut off from the green reconciling earth,
To starve into a blind ferocity
And glare unnatural; the very sky
(Dropping its bell-net down upon the sea
As if no human heart should 'scape alive,)
Bedraggled with the desolating salt,
Until it seemed no more that holy heaven
To which my father went. All new and strange;
The universe turned stranger, for a child.

(1:239–50)

Established as a version of the traditional epic voyage, this journey effectively alienates Aurora from her native land, her immediate family, her language and her self. Significantly, in a poem which is, as Christopher Keirstead demonstrates, 'grounded...in travel' and 'a poetics of cosmopolitanism' where Aurora 'forges...the ability to move between borders and to actively identify with specific others', this first journey is little short of terrifying.[9] For her father's country of origin rapidly becomes associated with 'frosty cliffs' (1:251) and fog, and the train which 'swept [her] on' (1:258), seeming powerless, exposes Aurora to a colourless world which she is unable to reconcile with her preconceptions of the land of Shakespeare. As she explicitly states, contrasting the vibrancy of her homeland and the seeming sterility of this new world, 'Italy/ Is one thing, England one' (1:626–7).

Moreover, as Aurora arrives at her aunt's house, there is little hope that the love associated with her parents might be rediscovered there. For in her aunt she finds a woman who is effectively the product of both the freezing nature of England and the rigid socio-political systems which the text overall critiques. As 'a masterpiece of tight restraint', in Glennis Stephenson's apposite phrasing,[10] Aurora's aunt functions as an agent of the Symbolic Order in its most austere, systematized and inhumane form as she seeks to shape the 'wild bird scarcely fledged' of her niece into one of those women that dominant society upholds as 'models to the universe' (1:310; 446). It is highly significant, then, that the accomplishments system to which Aurora is subjected and which is seemingly designed to eradicate both the individuality she has developed in Italy and that enquiring mind which will be essential to her future role as poet (1:385–454) is described using images which suggest both psychological *and* bodily violation. Most notably, this occurs in the horrific comparison of Aurora's experiences to the water-torture, 'flood succeeding flood/ To drench the incapable throat and split the veins' (1:468–9). Such shocking depictions of violence conducted against the body occur frequently in the text where, as with the earlier 'The Cry of the Children' and 'The Runaway Slave at Pilgrim's Point', they serve as a means of highlighting, in telling and disturbing ways, the tensions between the individual and dominant socio-political structures.

From the start, therefore, Aurora's English 'home' is associated with alienation, fragmentation and abuse, leaving her, as Matthew Reynolds rightly suggests in his comparison between this poem and *Casa Guidi Windows*, in an oppressed situation akin to 'the condition of "corpse-like" Italy under Austrian control.' Helen Cooper, too, has pointed to the ways in which, under her aunt's watch, Aurora's physical self appears to give way so that she 'almost sinks into female invalidism' – an important image for a poem (and a poet) so acutely aware of the politics of the body.[11] However, just as EBB's more overtly political poems foreground the possibilities of countering oppressive systems, so Aurora develops modes of resistance which become crucial to her subsequent subject formation. In contrast to the restrictions of her aunt's house, for example, and moving beyond her first negative impressions of her father's country, she comes to value aspects of the English landscape which operate, in true Wordsworthian fashion, as an enabling agent of transcendental spiritual release. In that time before the household stirs and, to draw upon the theories of Judith Butler, prescribed social identities have to be performed,[12] Aurora is able to 'escape/ As a soul from the body, out of doors' (1:693–4), breaking down the boundaries between inside and out, entrapment and liberation, and thereby 'open[ing] wide/ The window and my soul' (1:663–4). This new sense of release, increasingly associated with dissenting thought, is subsequently augmented by Aurora's discovery of her father's library, where his books – the seeming male 'canon' of authority and knowledge – offer a means of entering into new worlds of ideas and inspiration. Significantly, the language of awakening and rebirthing is particularly insistent in these sections as 'life creeps back', '[r]egenerating what I was' (1:560; 666). And then, most transformative of all, Aurora starts to read poetry, an experience which is described through a series of striking revolutionary images:

> As the earth
> Plunges in fury, when the internal fires
> Have reached and pricked her heart, and, throwing flat
> The marts and temples, the triumphal gates
> And towers of observation, clears herself
> To elemental freedom – thus, my soul,
> At poetry's divine first finger-touch,
> Let go conventions and sprang up surprised,
> Convicted of the great eternities
> Before two worlds.

> (1:846–54)

This is an astonishing passage, aligning the discovery of poetry with volcanic eruptions able to destroy the symbols of capitalism, religion and social control ('The marts and temples... towers of observation'). Poetry here is nothing less than a radical force, associated with both the rejection of conventions and the capacity to usher in a brave new world of 'elemental freedom' completely different to that which Aurora has known before. Certainly, this idea is further affirmed when Aurora starts to compose her own verse, an endeavour she describes, in a neat reworking of the earlier water torture image, as a 'violent flood' capable of '[a]bolish[ing] bounds' (1:961–2). Yet whilst the bursting of socio-political boundaries and conventions might be theoretically celebrated here, the remainder of *Aurora Leigh*, with what EBB termed its 'philosophical dreaming & digression' (*Correspondence* 9:304), demonstrates just how difficult this is to achieve in practice, particularly given the conflicts between the commitment to art and the commitment to socialist politics which underlie Aurora's relationship with Romney and the poem overall.

The first major exploration of these complex relations between art and politics occurs in the famous garden scene in Book 2 where Aurora asserts her right to professional independence over Romney's half-hearted marriage proposal. Crowning herself with ivy on her twentieth birthday – an act which recalls both Napoleon's crowning himself as Emperor in 1804 and, as critics such as Ellen Moers, Cora Kaplan and Angela Leighton have demonstrated, the crowning of the famous woman poet, Corinne, at the Capitol in Rome in Mme de Staël's 1807 novel of that name[13] – Aurora initially occupies a subject position of active, almost hubristic empowerment only to be quickly transfigured into an *inactive* and silenced art object by Romney's appearance. For in returning her book of poetry, Romney associates Aurora with a witch, thereby recalling one of the key transformations of the portrait of Aurora's mother in Book 1 and simultaneously highlighting his own anxieties concerning the potential power of the writing: 'I saw at once the thing had witchcraft in't/ Whereof the reading calls up dangerous spirits' (2:78–9). (Interestingly, Emily Dickinson employed a similar image in one of her tribute poems to EBB where she speaks of EBB's 'Tomes of solid Witchcraft'.[14]) Romney then proceeds to initiate a confrontational debate where he seeks to prioritize socialist philanthropic work (or his particular version of it) over the ideological work of poetry and art in general. Drawing upon those utilitarian arguments which, as Alan Sinfield and Joseph Bristow have demonstrated, increasingly characterized the dominant attitude to art across the nineteenth century,[15] Romney asserts that poetry is marginal to society's concerns and redundant in the treatment of its ills: 'The world's hard pressed...Who has time/...to sit upon a bank,/ And hear the cymbal tinkle in white hands?' (2:165; 168–70). Moreover, deploying some of the most reactionary Victorian views about *women's* poetry, and in somewhat ironic reflection on EBB's own career, Romney proceeds to condemn the way in which women write about personal and individual suffering rather than tackling the universal and general:

> The human race
> To you means, such a child, or such a man,
> You saw one morning waiting in the cold,
> Beside that gate, perhaps. You gather up
> A few such cases, and when strong sometimes
> Will write of factories and of slaves, as if
> Your father were a negro, and your son

> A spinner in the mills. All's yours and you,
> All, coloured with your blood, or otherwise
> Just nothing to you.
>
> . . . . . .
>
> Therefore, this same world,
> Uncomprehended by you, must remain
> Uninfluenced by you.—Women as you are,
> Mere women, personal and passionate,
> You give us doating mothers, and perfect wives,
> Sublime Madonnas, and enduring saints!
> We get no Christ from you, – and verily
> We shall not get a poet, in my mind.
>
> (2:189–98; 218–225)

Romney's critique of poetry, and especially women as practitioners, is clearly uncompromising and limited in outlook and is evidently rehearsed in the wake of his own commitment to socialism as a means of healing the world rather than an understanding of what art might achieve. As Cora Kaplan and Marjorie Stone have extensively detailed, EBB always hated the ideological basis of socialism and particularly the way in which she perceived socialist programmes to ignore that individuality which she believed to be crucial to intellectual, political and cultural development.[16] For as she wrote to Mitford about Louis Blanc in 1850:

> I love liberty so intensely that I hate Socialism. I hold it to be the most desecrating & dishonouring to Humanity, of all creeds. I would rather (for *me*) live under the absolutism of Nicholas of Russia, than in a Fourier-machine, with my individuality sucked out of me by a social air-pump. (*Mitford* 3:302).

The specific type of socialism highlighted here, Fourierism, was named after the French social theorist Charles Fourier (1772–1837) who advocated the transformation of society into small co-operative, self-sufficient communities called phalansteries, founded on an agrarian and handicraft economy and operating free from state intervention.[17] It is this particular model of socialist practice to which Romney subscribes and which, Aurora argues in an echo of EBB's own sentiments, is fundamentally flawed precisely because of its lack of concern with the individual person and their emotional and spiritual needs:

> It takes a soul,
> To move a body: it takes a high-souled man,
> To move the masses, even to a cleaner stye:
> It takes the ideal, to blow a hair's-breadth off
> The dust of the actual. – Ah, your Fouriers failed,
> Because not poets enough to understand
> That life develops from within.
>
> (2:479–85)

Whilst Aurora is evidently critical of Romney's politics here, she nevertheless also attempts to comprehend how his ideological allegiances may have been shaped by his own class and economic status. For after his father's death, Romney was made 'early master of Leigh Hall,/ Whereof the nightmare sate upon his youth/ Repressing all its seasonable delights' (1.516–18). As EBB repeatedly emphasizes throughout her writings, drawing in part on the ideas of Mary Wollstonecraft whose work she held in high esteem, power and status can be as damaging to those who possess them as they are to those who are subjected to them. Despite this attempt at empathy, however, Aurora clearly recognizes the problems which Romney's offer of marriage embodies at this particular stage. For Romney's couching his proposal in terms of requiring a helpmeet in social philanthropy rather than a partner in love (a proposal reminiscent of St John Rivers' offer to Jane Eyre in Charlotte Brontë's novel) is both problematic in its denial of individual emotion and anathema to a woman who argues strongly for the extension of the dominant Victorian work ethic to her own gender and to her understanding of poetry as meaningful employment. As Marjorie Stone has noted, debates surrounding women's work were highly topical in the mid-1850s as part of the wider concern with the 'woman question' and the roles and functions which (particularly middle-class) women should hold in society. (The campaigner for women's rights, Barbara Leigh Smith, published her controversial *Women and Work* just a few months after *Aurora Leigh*, for example.)[18] Aurora's arguments here therefore map onto an area of grave concern for the mid-Victorians as she emphasizes that writing poetry will enable her to have a greater chance of engendering social and political change than will Romney's vision of her 'sweep[ing]...barns' and 'keep[ing]...hospitals' (2:539). Indeed, as Aurora asserts, poetry is 'most necessary work/

As any of the economists' (2:459–60).

Aurora's commitment to becoming an established poet consequently sees her rebelling against both the oppressive bourgeois 'education' promoted by her aunt and the oppressive system of patriarchal ownership promoted by Romney's proposal. Recognizing that marrying Romney would, like the accomplishments system, violate both her physical and psychological self, she claims instead a new independence, asserting that 'I choose to walk at all risks' (2:106) – one of the many references to pedestrianism in the poem which, as Anne Wallace highlights,[19] indicate Aurora's growing confidence (just as it does for Lucy Snowe in Charlotte Brontë's *Villette* [1853]). It is therefore highly significant that, in a telling revision of the crowning scene which opens Book 2, Aurora defiantly picks up the 'soiled garland' of her poetic crown from the ground and reinstates it 'bitterly' on her head (2:809–10). Whereas the earlier ivy crown might be read as representing the death-centred poetry of Aurora's (and EBB's) female poetic predecessors, such as Hemans and Landon (see Chapter 1), her new 'soiled' crown represents the belief that poetry can engage with the world of political and social ills as well as, if not better than, Romney's version of socialism.

Aurora's pursuit of her career subsequently sees her undertaking the second crucial geographical shift in the poem, when, after her aunt's death and her effective expulsion from Leigh Hall by Romney, she moves to London. This move to the capital enables Aurora to establish herself at the heart of contemporary literary and political society, thereby opening up greater aesthetic possibilities. For here, in her 'close London life' (3:40), she works relentlessly in the archetypal garret associated with the penniless Romantic artist, writing both that undemanding poetry which will sell, thereby playing the literary marketplace, and that which helps her to shape a more radical poetics. Indeed, as a single woman in the metropolis, daring to be a writer (and a poet at that), Aurora challenges conventions, tests her belief systems, and starts to emerge as a more confident and independent woman as she literally writes herself into existence.

Significantly, it is also in London where Romney's socialist ambitions are most put to the test and particularly his belief that the proposed marriage to the working-class Marian Earle, '[t]his daughter of the people' (3:806), can help bring about a more generalized reconciliation between the classes. In this respect, of course, *Aurora Leigh* participates in those wider 'Condition of England' debates prevalent in the 1840s and 1850s which EBB had begun to tackle in 'The Cry of the Children' and 'Lady Geraldine's Courtship' and which were articulated more famously in novels such as Elizabeth Gaskell's *Mary Barton* (1848) and *North and South* (1855), Charlotte Brontë's *Shirley* (1849), Charles Kingsley's *Alton Locke* (1851) and Charles Dickens' *Hard Times* (1854). Indeed, it is this Condition-of-England aspect which Marjorie Stone has highlighted in her insightful reading of *Aurora Leigh* as an overlooked example of mid-Victorian sage writing (a genre which traditionally excludes women writers).[20] The way in which EBB represents the working classes in this poem, though, and the ideological assumptions underpinning these representations, has often been the site of sustained critical dispute, most notably in the readings by Cora Kaplan and Deirdre David. For Marian's background as it is narrated in Book 3, significantly through Aurora's words rather than her own, is one of over-riding brutality at the hands of a people who, in Aurora's middle-class language and perception, 'sin so, curse so, look so, smell so' (3:808). Having been dragged around the country in 'this tramping life', beaten by her drunken father, and only just escaping being prostituted by her mother to a man 'with beast's eyes/ That seemed as they would swallow her alive' (3:1032; 1050–1), Marian is eventually 'saved' by Romney in a scene which appears to construct him as a benevolent Christ-like figure (3:1198–1215). Yet at this stage Marian is viewed by Romney as little more than a symbol of his desire to '[c]ompress the red lips of this gaping wound' of class difference (4:127), one of the many figurings of social ills as diseased, fragmented or monstrous bodies which litter this text and many of EBB's other political writings.

As Rod Edmond has perceptively argued, however, the function of the cross-class marriage trope in *Aurora Leigh* is significantly different from that in other Victorian texts such as *Jane Eyre* (1847) or Arthur Hugh Clough's *The Bothie of Tober-na-Vuolich* (1848) where the marriage operates principally, if not always unproblematically, as an act of closure and resolution. Rather, in *Aurora Leigh*, 'the cross-class marriage is attempted in mid-narrative...[so that] its difficulties and self-deceptions [can be] explored.'[21] It is the antagonism in the church itself that most clearly evidences the exploration of these 'difficulties' and 'self-deceptions', in a scene which, Deirdre David suggests, 'calls to mind Hogarthian London' in its 'stunningly visual depiction'.[22] It is also this scene which has caused most critical consternation as the working classes are constructed as sub-human, 'pour[ing] down' to Pimlico, 'clogg[ing]' the streets and 'oozing' down the aisle (4:545; 553). Without doubt, Aurora's language here is particularly judgemental and bigoted as she surveys the assembled crowd:

> What an ugly crest
> Of faces rose upon you everywhere
> From that crammed mass! you did not usually
> See faces like them in the open day:
> They hide in cellars, not to make you mad
> As Romney Leigh is. – Faces! – O my God,
> We call those, faces? men's and women's...ay,
> And children's; – babies, hanging like a rag
> Forgotten on their mother's neck, – poor mouths,
> Wiped clean of mother's milk by mother's blow
> Before they are taught her cursing
>
> .   .   .   .
>
> Those, faces? 't was as if you had stirred up hell
> To heave its lowest dreg-fiends uppermost
> In fiery swirls of slime...

(4:569–79; 587–9)

As Aurora depicts them here, the working classes constitute a dangerous overwhelming tide of grotesque gothic horrors, emerging at night as some kind of Freudian return of the repressed and judged to be the seemingly inevitable outcome of a lack of family support and maternal caring. For in a poem which repeatedly comes back to the importance of mothering and which picks up on the idea of 'political mothering' explored in a number of EBB's earlier political poems (see Chapter 4), the mothers here are neglectful, abusive and violent. Moreover, in the scenes following Marian's jilting of Romney, where it is suspected that she has been killed in a middle-class conspiracy '[b]ecause she's poor and of the people' (4:845), the working classes are further reduced, in Cora Kaplan's phrasing, to 'a lumpen motley of thieves, drunkards, rapists and childbeaters.'[23]

Deirdre David has suggested that the problems of representation here, which 'seem to congeal in a brutal image of the dismembered body/social state', stem from the fact that EBB had little or no direct engagement with the working classes except on the one occasion when she went to Shoreditch to rescue her spaniel, Flush, from dog thieves (a point made by Virginia Woolf some fifty years earlier in her parodic 'biography' of EBB's pet).[24] However, there may be ways in which more subtle analyses of what EBB is doing here can be suggested, for as Marjorie Stone notes, many of the depictions of the working classes which EBB employs were common literary tropes in Condition-of-England works of the period, suggesting that scenes such as this one might function as part of what Cora Kaplan terms the text's 'overlapping sequence of dialogues with other texts, other writers.'[25] Moreover, as Stone proceeds to argue, in addition to EBB's engagement with this 'collective discourse of the poor', it is highly significant that Aurora's construction of the masses through what appears to be offensive and degrading imagery occurs at a relatively early stage in her development.[26] Given the novelistic techniques which EBB draws upon in this poem, including the development narrative of the *bildungsroman/künstlerroman*, we witness here not a vatic voice of authority and fixed opinion, but the voice of a protagonist who will move on to change her ideological position and revise her views, particularly through her relationship with Marian. Indeed, in a manner typical of the wider political debates underpinning this text, Aurora adopts a stance and is then forced to modify or rethink it given new experience. Rather than assigning class prejudice to EBB herself, then, it might be possible to argue that EBB is *critiquing* her protagonist's views at this stage, as she does later with Aurora's initial attitudes towards Marian's child.

Building on Stone's observations, it is also important to note that at this point of the text Aurora is critical of the *middle* classes as well, constructing many of the congregation as manipulative, money-grasping and deceitful, particularly in their dismissal of

Marian as an ignorant fallen woman: 'They say the bride's a mere child, who can't read,/ But knows the things she shouldn't, with wide-awake/ Great eyes' (4:645–7). Certainly, the middle classes are keen to suggest that philanthropic acts and discussion of '[t]his modern question of the poor' should remain at a distance, unsullied by realities:

> You've seen Prince Albert's model lodging-house?
> Does honour to his Royal Highness. Good!
> But would he stop his carriage in Cheapside
> To shake a common fellow by the fist...'
>
> (4:663; 665–8)

EBB therefore highlights that whilst Romney's socialist project is highly problematic in its agenda, the wider middle-class attitude is equally misguided, founded upon acute class prejudice and lacking any regard for the dignity of the individual. For whilst the middle-class congregation view Romney's marriage as 'anarchical' (4:696), they themselves have no solution to the problems of the Condition of England (a pattern which, as Josephine M. Guy emphasizes, is fundamental to many mid-nineteenth-century social-problem texts).[27] Indeed, both Romney's 'school/ Of philanthropical self-sacrifice', as Aurora terms it (4:1003–4), and the middle-class ignorance as it is depicted here, are complicit in the political and social ills which the text as a whole interrogates. As Elizabeth Gaskell emphasizes in her Condition-of-England fiction, it is this class antagonism and mutual distrust which needs to be resolved in order to bring about social change. And in another parallel with Gaskell's work, it is the outsider figure, Marian, rather than any man-made system, which will galvanize the new awareness necessary for the development of a new political order.

Following the aborted wedding and Marian's departure from the text, Aurora's subsequent narrative sees EBB tackling the period's growing concern with the figure of the fallen woman. For as EBB wrote at the time of the military conflict in the Crimea: 'War, war! It is terrible certainly. But there are worse plagues, deeper griefs, dreader wounds than the physical. What of the forty thousand wretched women in this city [London]? The silent writhing of them is to me more appalling than the roar of cannons.'[28] The fate of the fallen woman driven onto the streets through economic necessity, which EBB significantly identifies here as a 'wound' in the body of society, was of course the subject of many empathetic literary representations in the mid-nineteenth century, ranging from Gaskell's *Mary Barton* (1848) and *Ruth* (1853) – the latter a text which EBB viewed as 'strong and healthy at once, teaching a moral frightfully wanted in English society'[29] – to Christina Rossetti's 'Goblin Market' (1862), Dante Gabriel Rossetti's 'Jenny' (1870) and Augusta Webster's 'A Castaway' (1870). *Aurora Leigh* therefore participates in a tradition of awareness-raising on this issue, but again Aurora has to fight her middle-class prejudices and develop that more holistic view which, as EBB identifies from *An Essay on Mind* onwards, is necessary for political change. Significantly, however, this process occurs not in England but in *France*, when Aurora stops in Paris on her journey back to Italy. Indeed, in contrast to many critical accounts which emphasize *Aurora Leigh* as negotiating a series of seeming oppositions between Italy and England, I want to argue here that it is France, '[t]his poet of the nations' as Aurora terms it (6:54), which is the most important location for the text and its politics overall and which offers the greatest opportunities for social and political transformation.

On her initial arrival in Paris, Aurora celebrates the beauties of the capital in startling imagery:

> ...the terraced streets,
> The glittering boulevards, the white colonnades
> Of fair fantastic Paris who wears trees
> Like plumes, as if man made them, spire and tower
> As if they had grown by nature, tossing up
> Her fountains in the sunshine of the squares,
> As if in beauty's game she tossed the dice,
> Or blew the silver-down-balls of her dreams
> To sow futurity with seeds of thought
> And count the passage of her festive hours.
>
> .   .   .   .   .
> ...trade is art, and art's philosophy,
> In Paris.

(6:79–88; 96–7)

An intriguing collapsing-together occurs here – of the manmade and the natural, trade and art, art and philosophy – which is characteristic of the poem's overall concern with breaking boundaries and resisting categorization. And it is here, as Aurora wanders through the flower market, that Marian's face emerges out of the crowd like a symbolic return of the dead. Eager to hear Marian's story, then, Aurora leads her towards the place where she is staying, Marian following '[a]s if I led her by a narrow plank/Across devouring waters, step by step' (6:482–3). But when Marian realizes the impossibility of leaving her child alone, they retrace their path, this time with Aurora following 'as by a narrow plank/Across devouring waters' (6:501–2). As Margaret Reynolds suggests, this repeated journey 'marks the reversal of authority that takes place in terms of Aurora and Marian's relationship. First Aurora leads by virtue of intellect and status; then Marian leads by authority of experience and knowledge.'[30] Further, this repeated motif works to indicate both the gulf between the classes that needs to be bridged and the need for Aurora to challenge inherited modes of thought if she is to empathize in full with Marian's alienated situation. For as Aurora follows Marian through the dark and forbidding streets of the Paris slums – a journey which takes the place of the traditional descent into the underworld in Book Six of classical epics like the *Aeneid* and *Odyssey*, and which simulta-neously draws upon the French realist novelists that EBB was avidly reading (Honoré de Balzac, George Sand, Eugène Sue, Frédéric Soulié) – Marian recounts how she was sold into sexual slavery by Lady Waldemar and her female servant in one of the most acute representations of the exploitation of one class by another, and one woman by another, in Victorian literature. And it is arguably at this point that Aurora's greatest growth occurs. For initially Aurora is so horrified by Marian's status as single mother, believing her baby to represent '[i]nstead of honour [and] blessing, merely shame' (6:355), that she con-demns her in relentlessly unforgiving rhetoric:

> 'Ay! the child is well enough,'
> I answered. 'If his mother's palms are clean
> They need be glad of course in clasping such;
> But if not, I would rather lay my hand,
> Were I she, on God's brazen altar-bars
> Red-hot with burning sacrificial lambs,
> Than hold the sacred curls of such a child.'

(6:617–23)

It is Marian's subsequent revelation of her rape, however, where she tells how 'man's violence,/ Not man's seduction, made me what I am' (6:1226–7) and where, as Roy Gridley points out, the many ellipses in the telling indicate 'the limits of language in this description,'[31] that galvanizes Aurora's new understanding. Indeed, Marian is effectively transfigured in this scene from her position beyond the pale of society, hidden away with her 'filthy secret' (7:74), into a beatified saint, standing in glory with her child as the symbol of hope for a politically-secure and socially-inclusive future (an image which recalls EBB's description of her own son at the end of *Casa Guidi Windows*). To understand the politics of the fallen woman, the text radically argues, is to view the purity embodied in her, in the face of which all must be humbled:

> 'Defiled'
> I wrote? 'defiled' I thought her? Stoop,
> Stoop lower, Aurora! get the angels' leave
> To creep in somewhere, humbly, on your knees,
> Within this round of sequestration white
> In which they have wrapped earth's foundlings, heaven's elect.
>
> (7:389–94)

As Kate Lawson and Lynn Shakinovsky have observed in *The Marked Body*, their study of domestic violence in Victorian literature, 'the body of Marian ... is, at various points of the narrative, hurt, persecuted, despised, beaten, raped, and left for dead.'[32] Although Aurora's body is also constantly figured in terms of cutting and torturing in order to depict the impact of oppressive systems, Marian *literally* becomes the palimpsest upon which *Aurora Leigh*'s recurrent images of the fragmented body are most starkly written. Yet despite this – or rather, because of it – Marian's subsequent transfiguration suggests that the political redemption of society can best be achieved by those figures marginal to it, a vision which Charles Dickens had also promoted three years earlier in *Hard Times* with his depiction of the circus folk residing on the edge of Coketown. The culmination of all those exile figures who populate EBB's poetic works has therefore finally become central to the society which victimized her, an act which enables Marian to become increasingly outspoken and critical of dominant society. For like Aurora, who asserts 'I'm plain in speech, direct in purpose'

(8:1127), Marian comes to realize that speaking out plainly is the only way to engender positive change.

It is in Paris, therefore, where the fallen woman is redeemed, where Aurora comes to a new understanding of morality and cross-class relations, and where a new generous and empathetic relationship is set up upon which the rest of the text is dependent. Moreover, it is significantly in Paris that Aurora comes to a new awareness of the possibilities of art, enabling EBB, as Carol T. Christ highlights, to enter directly into 'contemporary aesthetic debates'.[33] For here Aurora realizes that the urban matrix, whether Paris, London or another city, is the only real focus for a work of art dealing with 'this live, throbbing age' (5:203). Indeed, just before she encounters Marian, Aurora makes an impassioned plea for the poet not to ignore the 'inartistic' in the urban world but rather, as with the scientist or surgeon who revels in deformed bodies, 'spend[ing] raptures upon perfect specimens/ Of un-durated veins, distorted joints' (6:175–6), to rethink traditional concepts of beauty, be bold enough to look 'into the swarthiest face of things' (6:148) and celebrate humankind in all its forms. Such is the new democratic poetics promoted by the woman poet who speaks for the modern world.

Yet there also seems to be something else going on here with the construction of Marian. For whilst critics have drawn attention to the associations of Marian's name with the Virgin Mary and Mary Magdalene, thereby forging a connection with the Magdalene figure at the base of the cross in *The Seraphim*, attention has not been paid to her name's associations with Marianne, the national emblem of the new French Republic and the allegorical figure of freedom and reason as it is depicted, for example, in Delacroix's *Liberty Leading the People* (1830). As Maurice Agulhon has documented, this image of revolutionary defiance, who represented the break with the corruption of the *ancien régime* and who embodied the dawning of the new age (a dawning also suggested in EBB's 'Aurora'), was named Marianne in 1792 during the First Republic.[34] It is extremely unlikely that such a politically-alert Francophile as EBB would employ the anglicized version of the name by coincidence. If we then follow this reading through, Aurora's taking Marian and all she represents back with her to Italy can be interpreted as representing the hope that the political freedom embodied in the new France could be recreated in an Italy pursuing unification, national self-agency and liberation from the Austrian occupier, that 'boar' which 'rake[s] up our grape/ And olive-gardens with his tyrannous tusk' as Aurora puts it (8:100; 105-6). Marian therefore becomes the symbol of a new political future in multiple ways and crucial to the formation of a meaningful home on many levels.

Significantly, in a poem which constantly reads notions of motherhood in political terms, Aurora initially expresses her return to Italy in terms of a return to the nurturing mythic mother: 'do you feel to-night', she addresses the country, 'The urgency and yearning of my soul,/ As sleeping mothers feel the sucking babe/ And smile?' (5:1268–71). And yet, after Aurora's coming to a new awareness in Paris, the actual journey to Italy is one which rather prioritizes the *modern* as Aurora and Marian travel by train 'in a roar of steam' down through France:

> Lyons dropped
> A spark into the night, half trodden out
> Unseen. But presently the winding Rhone
> Washed out the moonlight large along his banks
> Which strained their yielding curves out clear and clean
> To hold it, – shadow of town and castle just blurred
> Upon the hurrying river.
>   .   .   .   .   .   .
>   So we passed
> The liberal open country and the close,
> And shot through tunnels, like a lightening-wedge
> By great Thor-hammers driven through the rock,
> Which, quivering through the intestine blackness, splits,
> And lets it in at once: the train swept in
> Athrob with effort, trembling with resolve,
> The fierce denouncing whistle wailing on
> And dying off smothered in the shuddering dark,
> While we, self-awed, drew troubled breath, oppressed
> As other Titans, underneath the pile
> And nightmare of the mountains. Out, at last,
> To catch the dawn afloat upon the land!
> – Hills, slung forth broadly and gauntly everywhere,
> Not crampt in their foundations, pushing wide
> Rich outspreads of the vineyards and the corn...
>
>   (7:418–24; 429–44)

This is an astonishing depiction, combining elements of the sublime and the beautiful, the sense of the fecund landscape and the claustrophobia of the tunnel, in lines of great energy and propelling metre which effectively capture the speed and movement of the train. Indeed, with its celebration of the modern, even in its revisioning of classical figures, this passage powerfully enacts the journey which takes Aurora into a new world where she is able to challenge dominant thinking about politics and femininity more radically than at any other stage in the text. (The earlier 'Lady Geraldine's Courtship' similarly connects the modernity of the train with new, more radical thinking: see Chapter 3.) For as Angela Leighton argues, in taking the conventionally fallen woman to live with her as companion, Aurora establishes 'an ideological league of women defying, both in practice and in word, the divisions of their society.'[35] As both escape the marginal attic spaces they have previously inhabited in order to live in a villa on Bellosguardo overlooking Florence and the Arno, Aurora and Marian are able to reconfigure their position as exiles from the political structures of the 'chill north' (6:307) into a mutually-supportive relationship freed from previously imposed social identities. Here, then, in their alternative family unit, where two mothers replace the nominal nuclear structure, Marian is transformed from 'fallen woman' into pastoral heroine whilst Aurora consolidates her power as independent professional writer. Consequently, as Barbara Dennis observes, the narrative serves to confirm EBB's argument that 'personal commitment with individuals is more important than a social programme.'[36]

Yet this transition to a new state of being is not unproblematic for Aurora, since it again involves a significant rethinking of her previous relations and ways of viewing the world. In order to fund her journey back to the motherland, Aurora has had to sell her father's books, the discovery of which was one of the key moments of resistance and self-discovery for the young woman living in the austerity of her aunt's house. And when she arrives in Italy, she seeks out the childhood cottage she shared with her father, only to find it nearly buried by 'lingots of ripe Indian corn', reclaimed by nature and occupied by a girl platting straw and a group of 'lads...busy with their staves' as they strip the leaves from mulberry trees to provide food for silkworms

(7:1124; 1135). Whilst this symbolic return to the now destroyed family house might act as a cleansing process for the newly-successful woman poet, it nevertheless also leaves Aurora seemingly displaced and alienated as a 'restless ghost' (7:1161), an image which recalls her initial arrival in England. Indeed, Sandra Gilbert's argument that Italy is an unproblematically positive experience for the protagonists of *Aurora Leigh*, in contrast to the negative experience of England, breaks down here.[37] For Aurora now finds herself unable to act or write given that, in Margaret Reynolds' analysis, she has 'left behind her father's country and language and with it, apparently, all claim to action and to speech.'[38] With the self threatening to fragment, then, Aurora comes to realize that she needs more than work and more than a supportive relationship with another woman, however radical and liberating a social position that might embody. Rather, what is required for the establishment of a cohesive home and a new socio-political order in terms of the dynamics of the text overall is love, and specifically a love configured from a place of gender equality.

Romney's return to the narrative when he arrives at Bellosguardo initiates a series of new revelations and under-standings for all three major protagonists. For Romney now recognises Aurora as 'My Italy of women' (8:358) and possesses a new awareness of the power of her published writing ('the book is in my heart,/ Lives in me, wakes in me, and dreams in me', 8:265-6). Further, he now also possesses an awareness of the limitations of his own commitment to socialist thinking as he explicitly articulates the naivety of his past projects:

> 'I was heavy then,
> And stupid, and distracted with the cries
> Of tortured prisoners in the polished brass
> Of that Phalarian bull, society,
> Which seems to bellow bravely like ten bulls,
> But, if you listen, moans and cries instead
> Despairingly, like victims tossed and gored
> And trampled by their hoofs. I heard the cries
> Too close: I could not hear the angels lift
> A fold of rustling air, nor what they said
> To help my pity. I beheld the world
> As one great famishing carnivorous mouth, –
> A huge, deserted, callow, blind bird Thing,

> With piteous open beak that hurt my heart,
> Till down upon the filthy ground I dropped,
> And tore the violets up to get the worms.
> Worms, worms, was all my cry: an open mouth,
> A gross want, bread to fill it to the lips,
> No more.'

(8:385–403)

Here Romney images society as the Phalarian Bull, an ancient torture device where victims were placed inside a metal bull-shaped vessel which was heated until it seemed to roar with the screams of those imprisoned. As Romney argues, he was effectively deafened by these cries and so concerned with the 'filthy ground' of the temporal world that he forgot to register that spiritual dimension which, as Aurora had argued in the garden scene in Book 2, is fundamental both to art and socio-political change. Moreover, Romney is now able to acknowledge the more general problems associated with those systems which he had previously prioritized:

> 'There's too much abstract willing, purposing,
> In this poor world. We talk by aggregates,
> And think by systems, and, being used to face
> Our evils in statistics, are inclined
> To cap them with unreal remedies
> Drawn out in haste on the other side the slate.'

(8:800–5)

Driven out by the working classes he tried to help in the phalanstery on his estate and blinded and maimed in the style of *Jane Eyre*'s Rochester – a comparison which reviewers quickly seized upon and which EBB adamantly denied was any form of conscious imitation[39] – Romney is literally punished by his system as Leigh Hall is destroyed in a grotesque image of Bakhtinian carnival. With all its symbols of patriarchal culture and authority destroyed in 'one blazing jest' by 'those wild beasts, yelling, cursing round' (8:976; 994), the House of Leigh, which both Romney and his aunt had attempted to use to manipulate Aurora, is annihilated so that only one staircase is left, a symbol, Romney suggests, 'of my life,/ Ascending, winding, leading up to nought!' (8:1034–5).

As EBB wrote to her sister-in-law, Sariana, she believed

Romney had to be blinded 'to be made to see; just as Marian had to be dragged through the uttermost debasement of circumstances to arrive at the sentiment of personal dignity.'[40] Suffering is therefore a fundamental part of EBB's thinking on individual development and the possibilities of political change that this can afford (as it also is in works like *The Seraphim*, 'The Cry of the Children' and 'The Runaway Slave at Pilgrim's Point'). And it is the new 'personal dignity' acquired by Marian which finally permits her to engender both the most workable approach towards social reform in this text and the establishment of a meaningful home. For as Romney proposes to Marian a second time, constructing himself now as a *failed* Christ-figure and Marian as '[t]he very lamb left mangled by the wolves/ Through my own bad shepherding' (8:1063–4), her rejection of him emphasizes both her new self-respect and integrity and her insight into the new social order about to be born – a social order where she will remain more pure as the illegitimate mother who conventional society condemns than she will as Romney's wife. Indeed, as Marjorie Stone emphasizes, EBB's use of Marian as the major source of wisdom in these final debates is highly radical in the way it 'subverts the phallocentric discourse of the prophetic and wisdom traditions' associated with sage writing.[41] In effect, then, Marian becomes a modern version of the traditional priest figure, able to bring Aurora and Romney together so that their previous conflicts on the nature of the relationship between politics and art can be renegotiated and fully worked through.

For as Romney points out to Aurora, 'We both were wrong that June-day' (8:552). Certainly, whilst Romney's previous commitment to the unworkable, collective socialist system is held up for greatest scrutiny in the poem's last two books, Aurora herself is not beyond reproach since her overarching commitment to art has meant that she has sacrificed the love which she now sees as being crucial to her total fulfilment and which the text proposes is central for society's development. As she tells Romney in Book 9:

> You only thought to rescue men
> By half-means, half-way, seeing half their wants,
> While thinking nothing of your personal gain.
> But I who saw the human nature broad

At both sides, comprehending too the soul's,
And all the high necessities of Art,
Betrayed the thing I saw, and wronged my own life
For which I pleaded. Passioned to exalt
The artist's instinct in me at the cost
Of putting down the woman's, I forgot
No perfect artist is developed here
From any imperfect woman.

(9:638–49)

Whilst this speech, along with Aurora's repeated statement that 'Art is much, but love is more' (9:656), might seem reactionary after her previous declarations about rejecting conventional femininity, the poem overall enacts, as Glennis Stephenson argues, a significant paradigm shift in thinking about relationships, away from the traditional male-orientated models seen in Book 2 towards a newly-structured definition at the close where both partners 'assume vital active roles, and...maintain autonomy as individuals.'[42] This is certainly a major progression from the types of relationship interrogated in EBB's earlier ballads and there is no indication that Aurora will forsake her hard-won independence in her new situation with Romney. Rather, as Dorothy Mermin suggests, Aurora succeeds in getting 'much more than the nineteenth-century marriage plot usually allows its heroines: love *and* work *and* fame *and* independence *and* power.'[43]

In the final pages of the text, then, Aurora and Romney, coming together through the union of their 'wedded souls' (9:882), outline a new political partnership for a potential new world, a partnership which emerges from the combination of that resistance to traditional systems of thought and gender expectations which Aurora has evidenced throughout and Romney's new awareness that 'Fourier's void,/ And Comte absurd, – and Cabet, puerile' (9:868-9) since none of these utopian schemes has any room for God.[44] Consequently, they seek to reconcile Romney's humanitarianism with Aurora's commitment to art as 'service' (9:915) in order to create a new approach which, with religion as foundation, will 'raise men's bodies still by raising souls' (9:853) and eventually 'blow all class-walls level as Jericho's' (9:932-3). Indeed, having both learned to temper their previous excesses, Aurora and Romney now see the way forward to a new politics which will be nothing short of completely transformative:

> The world's old,
> But the old world waits the time to be renewed,
> Toward which, new hearts in individual growth
> Must quicken, and increase to multitude
> In new dynasties of the race of men;
> Developed whence, shall grow spontaneously
> New churches, new œconomies, new laws
> Admitting freedom, new societies
> Excluding falsehood: HE shall make all new.

(9:941–9)

Here, in a passage which recalls Aurora's initial discovery of poetry in Book 1, EBB depicts the coming of the New Jerusalem as it is portrayed in John's *Revelations* and given renewed currency through contemporary millenarian and socialist thought. As Marjorie Stone has noted, it is, of course, highly ironic that the concept of the New Jerusalem was central to the socialist ideals which EBB critiques throughout *Aurora Leigh*.[45] And yet the Owenite agenda as Barbara Taylor documents it, of 'a wholesale assault on all relations of dominance and subordination' and a vision of 'perfect equality and perfect freedom at every level',[46] is one that fits well with the politics of the poem overall. Certainly, with its promotion of a female-initiated new political order, which eradicates previous tyrannies and systems of oppression through the establishment of new churches and new governments, *Aurora Leigh* seems to move much further than Deirdre David's reading suggests when she argues that the politics of the poem are essentially conservative and that '[w]oman's talent is made the attendant of conservative male ideals.'[47] Rather, the new world vision as it is mapped out here is dependent upon the dismantling of male-dominated political structures, sustained resistance to oppressive systems of thought, and the ideological work of a fallen woman and a female poet, thereby offering, as Rebecca Stott suggests, 'a powerful counter-future to Carlyle's thunderous pessimism about the present age.'[48] And it is within this new world that Aurora Leigh, EBB's most complex and intriguing protagonist and the figure whom Virginia Woolf called 'the true daughter of her age',[49] finds that combination of spiritual, emotional and political stabilities for which the speakers and protagonists of her other poems are continually seeking. Here, in the poem which Robert Browning had correctly predicted would be a 'fearless fresh living work' (*Correspondence* 10:118) and which repeatedly breaks conventions by 'rushing into drawingrooms & the like, "where angels fear to tread"' (*Correspondence* 10:102–3), EBB is at last able to envisage a suitable home for the intellectual woman in the modern world.

Conclusion:
The Exile and the Empty Home

Over the course of this book, I have examined the recurrent concern with the notion of 'home' as it is explored in EBB's poetry, both in terms of poetics and subject matter. As I argued in Chapter 1, EBB's own search for a home in relation to literary traditions and inherited models of the poet led her to develop what was often a highly innovative and experimental poetics through which she increasingly dedicated herself to the interrogation of contemporary social and political concerns. In subsequent chapters, I have then explored the concept of the search for a home as it is undertaken by the speakers and protagonists in a wide range of EBB's works. This home is defined in multiple ways – as a spiritual home, an emotional home or a political home – but repeatedly both the home itself and the (often illusory) state of security associated with it are unavailable or unattainable. Indeed, time and again EBB's speakers and protagonists are left in a state of exile – from God and religious certainty, from love and a meaningful relationship, or from supportive political structures and an inclusive, liberal nation state. As I suggested in Chapter 5, it is only in the long, discursive novel-poem, *Aurora Leigh*, that the search for a creative and supportive home is rewarded when Aurora eventually achieves a position in Italy which brings together a relationship based on equality and mutual respect, professional esteem, religious security, and the potential for social change through the combination of art and politics.

And yet the notion of the stable and secure home which *Aurora Leigh* finally promotes is only a temporary phenomenon in EBB's body of poetry. For in the majority of the poems which

EBB composed after *Aurora Leigh* (she was to live for another five years until 1861), the focus on instability, fragmentation and lack of security which characterized her work of the 1820s to the 1840s becomes predominant once more. In *Poems Before Congress* (1860), for example, a volume named after an international conference on the Italian Question which never took place, EBB continues the interrogation of the politics of unification she had started with *Casa Guidi Windows*, but in a series of much shorter poems which at times take radically different stances in order to articulate EBB's changing opinions on the *Risorgimento*. Whilst 'Napoleon III in Italy' appears to hero-worship the leader, for example, viewing him as the potential 'Sublime Deliverer' of Italy from Austrian control (l.94) and seemingly defending his autocratic politics if this delivery is to be achieved, 'A Tale of Villafranca' expresses EBB's overriding despair when Napoleon sells out to Austria in 1859. This despair is then augmented in other poems in the collection which critique both the populous for their reactionary political stance ('An August Voice') and the Pope, Pius IX, for abandoning his spiritual care of the people ('Christmas Gifts'). Indeed, the establishment of a political homeland seems further away than ever, although EBB seems to locate hope in cross-nation cooperation ('The Dance') and the power of women to intervene politically ('A Court Lady'). Under these conditions, 'Beautiful Italy' might eventually be able to 'Rise heroic and renovated' ('Italy and the World', ll.33–4).

In the final poem of the collection, however, the astonishing 'A Curse for a Nation', EBB shifts the focus away from Italy to America, reinforcing the idea of an oppressive nation state through a fierce denunciation of the slavery system which she had previously attacked in 'The Runaway Slave at Pilgrim's Point'. For here, an angel – that figure which is frequently associated with the need for a new socio-political awareness in EBB's writing – encourages the speaker to deliver a sharp attack against America, the supposed nation of the free which creates 'writhing bond-slaves' (l.63) in order to support its economy. As the angel states, 'A curse from the depths of womanhood/ Is very salt, and bitter, and good' (ll.49–50). In the last poem of the final collection that EBB herself oversaw, therefore, the concept of a home in the nation state remains as illusive as ever.

Although EBB would live to see her desire for Italian

unification almost completed, dying within three months of the establishment of the new Italian parliament, the poems she left unpublished and which Robert collected together as *Last Poems* (1862) still focus predominantly on the problems of the *Risorgimento* in works such as 'First News from Villafranca', 'The Forced Recruit', 'A View Across the Roman Campagna, 1861' and 'Summing Up in Italy'. Indeed, whilst EBB celebrates the leader of the nearly-unified Italy in 'King Victor Emmanuel Entering Florence', the dominant tone of these Italian poems is one of loss and despair. This is felt most acutely in one of EBB's most intriguing poems, 'Mother and Poet', a dramatic mono-logue whose speaker, the key *Risorgimento* poet Laura Savio, anguishes over her promotion of the nationalist cause when it has led to the deaths of both her sons in battle. Her home is now literally deserted (the father is significantly missing throughout), which leaves her questioning, 'when Italy's made, for what end is it done/ If we have not a son?' (ll.74–5). Both family and nation subsequently seem dispossessed of a future. When these Italian poems are then read alongside the other poems in the collection – works such as 'Void in Law', 'A False Step', 'Bianca Among the Nightingales' and 'Lord Walter's Wife', which return to the patterns of betrayal, double standards and power games characterizing the early ballads; 'De Profundis' which articu-lates EBB's grief at the death of her brother; and 'A Song for the Ragged Schools of London', which continues to critique aspects of the Condition of England – the overarching emphasis of *Last Poems* appears to be the denial of those emotional, familial, religious and political securities for which EBB's poetic speakers and protagonists have been constantly searching across her career. Indeed, as EBB's work overall suggests, until those structures of oppression which repeatedly alienate individuals, sectors of society or whole nations are challenged, and the 'evil' which is 'in the system' remedied (*Correspondence* 11:43), we may very well be left, as the speaker of 'Parting Lovers' terms it, with 'empty heart and home' (l.56).

Notes

PREFACE

1. Alethea Hayter, *Elizabeth Barrett Browning* (Writers and their Work, London: Longman, 1965), p.29.
2. Virginia Woolf, 'Aurora Leigh', in Michèle Barrett (ed.), *Women and Writing* (London: Women's Press, 1979), p.134.
3. The 'loss' and 'recovery' of EBB's status in literary history is explored in detail in Marjorie Stone, *Elizabeth Barrett Browning* (Basingstoke: Macmillan, 1995), pp.189–228; and Tricia Lootens, *Lost Saints: Silence, Gender, and Victorian Literary Canonization* (Charlottesville: University Press of Virginia, 1996), pp.116–57. See also Simon Avery and Rebecca Stott, *Elizabeth Barrett Browning* (London: Longman, 2003), pp.1–22.
4. *Aurora Leigh*, ed. Margaret Reynolds (New York and London: Norton, 1996), p.ix.
5. Lorna Sage, review in *Times Literary Supplement*. Quoted on the dustjacket of the Women's Press edition.
6. I would like to thank Vicky Greenaway from the Browning Society for inviting me to give this talk, and Mike and Jann Lewis for allowing the event to be held in what is now their private house.

CHAPTER 1 THE SHAPING OF A POETICS

1. *Athenaeum* June 1850, p.585.
2. For further discussion of these ideas, see Simon Avery and Rebecca Stott, *Elizabeth Barrett Browning* (London: Longman, 2003), pp.57–60.
3. Rowena Fowler, 'On Not Knowing Greek', *The Classical Journal* 78 (1983), 337–49, p.339.
4. Marjorie Stone, *Elizabeth Barrett Browning* (Basingstoke: Macmillan, 1995), pp.49–93.
5. Quotations taken from Everard H. King's reprinting of the poem in *James Beattie's The Minstrel and the Origins of Romantic Autobiography*

(Lampeter: Edwin Mellen Press, 1992).

6. Joseph Bristow (ed.), *The Victorian Poet: Poetics and Persona* (London: Croom Helm, 1987), pp.1–26; Alan Sinfield, *Alfred Tennyson* (Oxford: Basil Blackwell, 1986), pp.11–56; Carol T. Christ, 'Introduction' to Richard Cronin, Alison Chapman and Antony H. Harrison (eds), *A Companion to Victorian Poetry* (Oxford: Blackwell, 2002), pp.1–21.

7. Wordsworth and Coleridge, *Lyrical Ballads*, ed. R. L. Brett and A. R. Jones (London: Routledge, 1988), p.259. Quotations are from the expanded 1802 Preface.

8. Jerome McGann, *The Romantic Ideology* (Chicago: University of Chicago Press, 1989), esp. chapter 8.

9. Wordsworth and Coleridge, *Lyrical Ballads*, pp.244; 254.

10. J. R. Watson, *English Poetry of the Romantic Period* (London: Longman, 1985), pp.1–24.

11. Jennifer Wallace, *Shelley and Greece: Rethinking Romantic Hellenism* (Basingstoke: Macmillan, 1997), p.192.

12. In 'The Poet and the Bird', the speaker emphasizes that the poet's song resonates from his grave despite the fact that (or maybe because) he has been exiled by the community. Samantha Matthews has discussed the significance of nineteenth-century poets' graves in *Poetical Remains: Poets' Graves, Bodies, and Books in the Nineteenth Century* (Oxford: Oxford University Press, 2004).

13. Percy Bysshe Shelley, 'A Defence of Poetry' [written 1821; published 1840], in *The Norton Anthology of English Literature*, Volume Two, ed. M. H. Abrams and Stephen Greenblatt (New York: Norton, 2000), p.802.

14. Avery and Stott, *Elizabeth Barrett Browning*, pp.46–7.

15. Carlyle, 'The Hero as Poet' in Michael K. Goldberg, Joel J. Brattin, and Mark Engel (eds), *On Heroes, Hero-Worship, and the Heroic in History* (Berkeley: University of California Press, 1993), pp.67–97.

16. Translated by Charlotte Porter and Helen A. Clarke, *The Complete Works of Elizabeth Barrett Browning* (New York: Thomas Y. Cromwell, 1900), volume 1, p.244.

17. Quoted in John R. Greenfield (ed.), *British Romantic Poets, 1789–1832* (Detroit: Gale, 1990), p.28.

18. For a fascinating discussion of EBB's relationship to fame, see Eric Eisner's chapter 'Elizabeth Barrett Browning and the Energies of Fandom' in his book-length study, *Nineteenth-Century Poetry and Literary Celebrity* (Basingstoke: Palgrave Macmillan, 2009).

19. Letter to George Lewes, 12 January 1848. *The Letters of Charlotte Brontë: 1848–1851*, ed. Margaret Smith (Oxford: Oxford University Press, 2000), p.10.

20. See Alethea Hayter's astute analysis of EBB's experiments in poetic technique in *Mrs Browning: A Poet's Work and Its Setting* (London:

Faber, 1962), chapter 3.

21. Simon Avery, 'Telling It Slant: Promethian, Whig, and Dissenting Politics in Elizabeth Barrett's Poetry of the 1830s', *Victorian Poetry* 44.4 (2006), 405–24.

22. Linda M. Lewis, *Elizabeth Barrett Browning's Spiritual Progress: Face to Face with God* (Columbia: University of Missouri Press, 1998), p.20.

23. *Prometheus Bound*, trans. James Scully and C. J. Herington (New York: Oxford University Press, 1975), p.11.

24. Karen Dieleman, 'Elizabeth Barrett Browning's Religious Poetics: Congregationalist Models of Hymnist and Preacher', *Victorian Poetry* 45.2 (2007), 135–57.

25. Helen Cooper, *Elizabeth Barrett Browning: Woman and Artist* (Chapel Hill: University of North Carolina Press, 1988), p.42.

26. Tricia Lootens, 'Hemans and Home: Victorianism, Feminine "Internal Enemies", and the Domestication of National Identity', in Angela Leighton (ed.), *Victorian Women Poets: A Critical Reader* (Oxford: Blackwell, 1996), pp.1–23; and Emma Mason, *Women Poets of the Nineteenth Century* (Writers and their Work; Tavistock: Northcote House, 2006).

27. Anne K. Mellor, 'The Female Poet and the Poetess: Two Traditions of British Women's Poetry, 1780–1820', in Isobel Armstrong and Virginia Blain (eds), *Women's Poetry in the Enlightenment: The Making of a Canon* (Basingstoke: Macmillan, 1999), p.82.

28. For discussion of this idea, see Sandra Donaldson, 'Elizabeth Barrett's Two Sonnets to George Sand', in Sandra Donaldson (ed.), *Critical Essays on Elizabeth Barrett Browning* (New York: G. K. Hall, 1999). See also Joseph Phelan, *The Nineteenth-Century Sonnet* (Basingstoke: Macmillan, 2005).

29. Mary Sanders Pollock, *Elizabeth Barrett Browning and Robert Browning: A Creative Partnership* (Aldershot: Ashgate, 2003).

30. Alison Chapman, 'The Expatriate Poetess', in Alison Chapman (ed.), *Victorian Women Poets* (Cambridge: Brewer, 2003), p.58.

31. Julia Markus, 'Introduction' to *Casa Guidi Windows* (Barre, Mass.: Imprint Society, 1977); Isobel Armstrong, '*Casa Guidi Windows*: Spectacle and Politics in 1851', in Alison Chapman and Jane Stabler (eds), *Unfolding the South: Nineteenth-Century British Women Writers and Artists in Italy* (Manchester: Manchester University Press, 2003), pp.51–69. See also Richard Cronin, '*Casa Guidi Windows*: Elizabeth Barrett Browning, Italy and the Poetry of Citizenship', in Chapman and Stabler, *ibid.*, pp.35–50.

32. Katherine Montwieler, 'Domestic Politics: Gender, Protest, and Elizabeth Barrett Browning's *Poems Before Congress*', *Tulsa Studies in Women's Literature* 24.2 (2005), 291–317; Elizabeth Woodworth, 'Elizabeth Barrett Browning, Coventry Patmore, and Alfred

Tennyson on Napoleon III: The Hero-Poet and Carlylean Heroics', *Victorian Poetry* 44.4 (2006), 543–60.

CHAPTER 2 THE SEARCH FOR A SPIRITUAL HOME

 1. Dorothy Mermin, *Elizabeth Barrett Browning: The Origins of a New Poetry* (Chicago: Chicago University Press, 1989), p.69.
 2. Julia Neuberger (ed.), *The Things That Matter: An Anthology of Women's Spiritual Poetry* (London: Kyle Cathie, 1992), p.2.
 3. Linda M. Lewis, *Elizabeth Barrett Browning's Spiritual Progress: Face to Face With God* (Columbia: University of Missouri Press, 1998); Karen Dieleman, 'Elizabeth Barrett Browning's Religious Poetics: Congregationalist Models of Hymnist and Preacher', *Victorian Poetry* 45.2 (2007), 135–57.
 4. Mark Knight and Emma Mason, *Nineteenth-Century Religion and Literature* (Oxford: Oxford University Press, 2006), p.21.
 5. Charles Lyell, *Principles of Geology*, Volume One [1830], ed. James A. Secord (London: Penguin, 1997), p.26.
 6. Dieleman, 'Elizabeth Barrett Browning's Religious Poetics', p.145.
 7. 'Telling It Slant: Promethian, Whig, and Dissenting Politics in Elizabeth Barrett's Poetry of the 1830s', *Victorian Poetry* 44.4 (2006), 405–24, p.419. I have rehearsed an earlier version of my argument on *The Seraphim* in this article.
 8. Rebecca Stott in Simon Avery and Rebecca Stott, *Elizabeth Barrett Browning* (London: Longman, 2003), p.72.
 9. Antony H. Harrison, *Victorian Poets and the Politics of Culture: Discourse and Ideology* (Charlottesville: University Press of Virginia, 1998), p.71.
10. The idea of the passive, 'feminized' Christ was employed by a number of nineteenth-century women writers as a way of regendering the Son of Man. A version of a female Christ figure can be found, for example, in Christina Rossetti's 'Goblin Market' (1862), Mary Elizabeth Coleridge's 'The Other Side of a Mirror' (1896) and Florence Nightingale's *Cassandra* (1852; published 1928). Helen Cooper (*Elizabeth Barrett Browning: Woman and Artist*, Chapel Hill: University of North Carolina Press, 1988, p.15), Dorothy Mermin (*Elizabeth Barrett Browning*, p.51), and Marjorie Stone (*Elizabeth Barrett Browning*, Basingstoke: Macmillan, 1995, p.72) have all rehearsed the idea of Prometheus representing the passive victim of patriarchal ideology.
11. Lewis, *Elizabeth Barrett Browning's Spiritual Progress*, p.45.
12. Cooper, *Elizabeth Barrett Browning*, p.30.
13. See, for example, Shirley Keeldar's anti-Miltonic speeches in

Charlotte Brontë's *Shirley* (1849), chapter 18.

14. Stone, *Elizabeth Barrett Browning*, p.77.
15. Dieleman, 'Elizabeth Barrett Browning's Religious Poetics', p.146.
16. See Antony H. Harrison, *Victorian Poets and Romantic Poems: Intertextuality and Ideology* (Charlottesville: University Press of Virginia, 1990), pp.127–34.
17. Corinne Davies has persuasively argued that this poem advocates Christianity as the key modern poetic subject. See 'Two of Elizabeth Barrett Browning's Pan Poems and Their After-Life in Robert Browning's "Pan and Luna"', *Victorian Poetry* 44.4 (2006), 561–70.

CHAPTER 3 THE SEARCH FOR AN EMOTIONAL HOME

1. Glennis Stephenson, *Elizabeth Barrrett Browning and the Poetry of Love* (Ann Arbor, Mich.: U.M.I. Research, 1989), p.29.
2. See Stephenson *ibid.*; Angela Leighton, *Victorian Women's Poetry: Writing Against the Heart* (Hemel Hempstead: Harvester Wheatsheaf, 1992), pp.80–91; Marjorie Stone, *Elizabeth Barrett Browning* (Basingstoke: Macmillan, 1995), chapter 3; Rebecca Stott in Simon Avery and Rebecca Stott, *Elizabeth Barrett Browning* (London: Longman, 2003), chapter 6.
3. Alethea Hayter, *Mrs Browning: A Poet's Work and Its Setting* (London: Faber, 1962), p.80.
4. In her 1831–2 diary, EBB called herself 'a worshipper' of the late-eighteenth-century gothic novelist, Ann Radcliffe, for example. *Diary by EBB: The Unpublished Diary of Elizabeth Barrett Browning, 1831–2*, ed. Philip Kelley and Ronald Hudson (Athens: Ohio University Press, 1969), p.51.
5. Rosemary Jackson, *Fantasy: The Literature of Subversion* (London: Methuen, 1981), p.25.
6. Eugenia DeLamotte, *Perils of the Night: Nineteenth-Century Feminist Gothic* (Oxford: Oxford University Press, 1990), p.vii.
7. Dorothy Mermin, *Elizabeth Barrett Browning: The Origins of a New Poetry* (Chicago: University of Chicago Press, 1989), p.72.
8. Delamotte, *Perils of the Night*, p.vii.
9. For insightful accounts of the politics of the literary annuals, which were often written by and for women, see Angela Leighton and Margaret Reynolds (eds), *Victorian Women Poets: An Anthology* (Oxford: Blackwell, 1995), pp.xxv–xxxiv; and Patricia Pulham, 'Victorian Women Poets and the Annuals', in Alison Chapman (ed.), *Victorian Women Poets* (Cambridge: Brewer, 2003), pp.9–31.
10. Virginia Radley, *Elizabeth Barrett Browning* (Boston: Twayne, 1972), p.55.

11. Mermin, *Elizabeth Barrett Browning*, p.71.
12. Stone, *Elizabeth Barrett Browning*, p.131.
13. Angela Leighton, *Elizabeth Barrett Browning* (Brighton: Harvester Wheatsheaf, 1986), p.96; Helen Cooper, *Elizabeth Barrett Browning: Woman and Artist* (Chapel Hill: University of North Carolina Press, 1988), p.97.
14. Stone, *Elizabeth Barrett Browning*, pp.108–9.
15. Leighton, *Victorian Women's Poetry*, p.87.
16. Stephenson, *Elizabeth Barrett Browning*, p.61.
17. In the 1840s Browning published many of his works, including early dramatic monologues, in a series of pamphlets called *Bells and Pomegranates*.
18. See, in particular, Cooper, *Elizabeth Barrett Browning*, pp.99–110; Mermin, *Elizabeth Barrett Browning*, pp.128–46; Barbara Neri, '*Cobridme de flores*: (Un)Covering Flowers of Portuguese and Spanish Poets in *Sonnets from the Portuguese*', *Victorian Poetry* 44.4 (2006), 571–83; Joseph Phelan, *The Nineteenth-Century Sonnet* (Basingstoke: Palgrave Macmillan, 2005); Stephenson, *Elizabeth Barrett Browning*, pp.69–89; Marjorie Stone, '*Monna Innominata* and *Sonnets from the Portuguese*: Sonnet Traditions and Spiritual Trajectories', in Mary Arseneau, Antony H. Harrison and Lorraine Janzen Kooistra (eds), *The Culture of Christina Rossetti: Female Poetics and Victorian Contexts* (Athens: Ohio University Press, 1999), pp.46–94.
19. Alison Chapman, 'Sonnet and Sonnet Sequence', in Richard Cronin, Alison Chapman and Antony H. Harrison (eds), *A Companion to Victorian Poetry* (Oxford: Blackwell, 2002), p.106.
20. Isobel Armstrong, *Victorian Poetry: Poetry, Poetics, Politics* (London: Routledge, 1993), p.356.

CHAPTER 4 THE SEARCH FOR A POLITICAL HOME

1. Simon Avery and Rebecca Stott, *Elizabeth Barrett Browning* (London: Longman, 2003), pp.33–6.
2. Dorothy Mermin, *Elizabeth Barrett Browning: The Origins of a New Poetry* (Chicago: Chicago University Press, 1989), p.38.
3. Roy Gridley, *The Brownings and France: A Chronicle with Commentary* (London: Athlone Press, 1982), p.50.
4. Helen Cooper, *Elizabeth Barrett Browning: Woman and Artist* (Chapel Hill: University of North Carolina Press, 1988), p.111.
5. Angela Leighton, *Victorian Women Poets: Writing Against the Heart* (Hemel Hempstead: Harvester Wheatsheaf, 1992), p.94.
6. Marjorie Stone offers a fascinating reading of the politics of cursing

in EBB's work in 'Cursing as One of the Fine Arts: Elizabeth Barrett Browning's Political Poems', *Dalhousie Review* 66:1–2 (1986), 155–73.

7. For more on the Barrett family's engagement with slavery, see Jeanette Marks, *The Family of the Barrett: A Colonial History* (New York: Macmillan, 1938), and R. A. Barrett, *The Barretts of Jamaica* (Waco, TX.: Armstrong Browning Library, 2000). For an intriguing fictionalized account, see Laura Fish, *Strange Music* (London: Jonathan Cape, 2008).

8. Alan Richardson, 'Slavery and Romantic Writing', in Duncan Wu (ed.), *Blackwell Companion to Romanticism* (Oxford: Blackwell, 1998), p.460.

9. Marjorie Stone, 'Elizabeth Barrett Browning and the Garrisonians: "The Runaway Slave at Pilgrim's Point", the Boston Female Anti-Slavery Society, and Abolitionist Discourse in the *Liberty Bell*', in Alison Chapman (ed.), *Victorian Women Poets* (Cambridge: Brewer, 2003), p.41.

10. Julia Markus, *Dared and Done: The Marriage of Elizabeth Barrett and Robert Browning* (London: Bloomsbury, 1995), p.92.

11. Cooper, *Elizabeth Barrett Browning*, p.112.

12. See Susanne Everett, *History of Slavery* (London: Grange Books, 1997), p.139.

13. Stone, 'Elizabeth Barrett Browning and the Garrisonians', p.49.

14. Cooper, *Elizabeth Barrett Browning*, p.114.

15. Deirdre David, *Intellectual Women and Victorian Patriarchy: Harriett Martineau, Elizabeth Barrett Browning, George Eliot* (London: Macmillan, 1987), p.139.

16. Linda M. Lewis, *Elizabeth Barrett Browning's Spiritual Progress: Face to Face With God* (Columbia: University of Missouri Press, 1998), p.191.

17. David, *Intellectual Women*, p.139.

18. Lincoln's 'House Divided' speech was given at Springfield, Illinois, on 16 June 1858.

19. Leighton, *Victorian Women Poets*, p.99.

20. Avery and Stott, *Elizabeth Barrett Browning*, pp.156–80. See also the insightful analyses by Mermin, *Elizabeth Barrett Browning*, pp.164–74; Joseph Phelan, 'Elizabeth Barrett Browning's *Casa Guidi Windows*, Arthur Hugh Clough's *Amours de Voyage*, and the Italian National Uprisings of 1847–9', *Journal of Anglo-Italian Studies* 3 (1993), 137–52; and Matthew Reynolds, *The Realms of Verse, 1830–1870: English Poetry in a Time of Nation-Building* (Oxford: Oxford University Press, 2001), pp.89–103.

21. Avery and Stott, *Elizabeth Barrett Browning*, p.175.

22. For more on EBB's engagement with the politics of motherhood, see Sandra Donaldson, '"Motherhood's Advent in Power": Elizabeth Barrett Browning's Poems About Motherhood', *Victorian Poetry*

18.1 (1980), 51–60; and Olivia Gatti Taylor, 'Written in Blood: The Art of Mothering Epic in the Poetry of Elizabeth Barrett Browning', *Victorian Poetry* 44.2 (2006), 153–64.

CHAPTER 5 RESTRUCTURING HOME: *AURORA LEIGH*

1. Marjorie Stone, *Elizabeth Barrett Browning* (Basingstoke: Macmillan, 1995), p.142.
2. Susan Stanford Friedman, 'Gender and Genre Anxiety: Elizabeth Barrett Browning and H.D. as Epic Poets', *Tulsa Studies in Women's Literature* 5.2 (1986), p.217.
3. Mary Sanders Pollock, *Elizabeth Barrett Browning and Robert Browning: A Creative Partnership* (Aldershot: Ashgate, 2003), p.178.
4. Quoted in *Aurora Leigh and Other Poems*, ed. Cora Kaplan (London: Women's Press, 1978), p.15.
5. Dickinson, 'The Soul has Bandaged moments –', l.13.
6. Dorothy Mermin, *Elizabeth Barrett Browning: The Origins of a New Poetry* (Chicago: University of Chicago Press, 1989), pp.190–2.
7. For consideration of this scene, see Sandra M. Gilbert and Susan Gubar, *The Madwoman in the Attic: The Woman Writer and the Nineteenth Century Literary Imagination* (New Haven: Yale University Press, 1979), pp.18–20; Mermin, *Elizabeth Barrett Browning*, pp.190–2; and Joyce Zonana, ' "The Embodied Muse": Elizabeth Barrett Browning's *Aurora Leigh* and Feminist Poetics', *Tulsa Studies in Women's Literature* 8.2 (1989), 241–62.
8. Helen Cooper, *Elizabeth Barrett Browning: Woman and Artist* (Chapel Hill: University of North Carolina Press, 1988), p.156.
9. Christopher Keirstead, 'A Bad Patriot?: Elizabeth Barrett Browning and Cosmopolitanism', *Victorians Institute Journal* 33 (2005), 69–95, p.70.
10. Glennis Stephenson, *Elizabeth Barrett Browning and the Poetry of Love* (Ann Arbor, Mich.: U.M.I. Research, 1989), p.94.
11. Matthew Reynolds, *The Realms of Verse, 1830–1870: English Poetry in a Time of Nation-Building* (Oxford: Oxford University Press, 2001), p.109; Cooper, *Elizabeth Barrett Browning*, p.159.
12. Judith Butler, *Gender Trouble* (London: Routledge, 1999), pp.171–90.
13. Ellen Moers, *Literary Women* (London: W. H. Allen, 1977), pp.173–210; *Aurora Leigh and Other Poems*, ed. Kaplan, pp. 17–22; Angela Leighton, *Victorian Women Poets: Writing Against the Heart* (Hemel Hempstead: Harvester Wheatsheaf, 1992), pp.30–4.
14. Dickinson, 'I think I was enchanted', l.29. On Dickinson's poems to EBB, see Betsy Erkkila, *The Wicked Sisters: Women Poets, Literary History, and Discord* (New York and Oxford: Oxford University

Press, 1992), pp.68–79; and Simon Avery (ed.), *Lives of Victorian Literary Figures: The Brownings* (London: Pickering and Chatto, 2004), pp.401–6.

15. Alan Sinfield, *Tennyson* (Oxford: Basil Blackwell, 1986), pp.11–21; Joseph Bristow (ed.), *The Victorian Poet: Poetics and Persona* (London: Croom Helm, 1987), pp.4–12.
16. *Aurora Leigh and Other Poems*, ed. Kaplan, pp.29–35; Stone, *Elizabeth Barrett Browning*, pp.147–52; 180–2.
17. See Fourier's *Théorie des quatres mouvements et des destinées générales* (1808), *Traité de l'association agricole domestique* (1822), and *Le Nouveau Monde Industriel* (1829–30).
18. Stone, *Elizabeth Barrett Browning*, pp.174–6.
19. Anne Wallace, ' "Nor in Fading Silks Compose": Sewing, Walking, and Poetic Labour in *Aurora Leigh'*, *ELH* 64.1 (1997), 223–56, esp. p.233ff.
20. Stone, *Elizabeth Barrett Browning*, p.138.
21. Rod Edmond, *Affairs of the Hearth: Victorian Narrative Poetry and the Ideology of the Domestic* (London: Routledge, 1988), p.162.
22. Deirdre David, *Intellectual Women and Victorian Patriarchy: Harriet Martineau, Elizabeth Barrett Browning, George Eliot* (London: Macmillan 1987), p.103.
23. *Aurora Leigh and Other Poems*, ed. Kaplan, p.12.
24. David, *Intellectual Women*, p.127; Virginia Woolf, *Flush* (London: Hogarth Press, 1933), chapter 4.
25. *Aurora Leigh and Other Poems*, ed. Kaplan, p.16; Stone, *Elizabeth Barrett Browning*, p.162–3.
26. Stone, *Elizabeth Barrett Browning*, p.163.
27. See Josephine M. Guy, *The Victorian Social-Problem Novel: The Market, the Individual and Communal Life* (Basingstoke: Macmillan, 1996).
28. Quoted in Alethea Hayter, *Mrs Browning: A Poet's Work and Its Setting* (London: Faber, 1962), p.181.
29. Quoted in *Aurora Leigh and Other Poems*, ed. Kaplan, p.25.
30. *Aurora Leigh*, ed. Margret Reynolds (New York and London: Norton, 1996), p.196, n.9.
31. Roy Gridley, *The Brownings and France: A Chronicle with Commentary* (London: Athlone Press, 1982), p.186.
32. Kate Lawson and Lynn Shakinovsky, *The Marked Body: Domestic Violence in Mid-Nineteenth-Century Literature* (Albany: State University of New York Press, 2002), p.108.
33. Carol T. Christ, 'Introduction', in Richard Cronin, Alison Chapman and Antony H. Harrison (eds), *A Companion to Victorian Poetry* (Oxford: Blackwell, 2002), p.11.
34. Maurice Agulhon, *Marianne into Battle: Republican Imagery and Symbolism in France, 1789–1800*, trans. Janet Lloyd (Cambridge:

Cambridge University Press, 1981).
35. Angela Leighton, *Elizabeth Barrett Browning* (Brighton: Harvester Wheatsheaf, 1986), p.148.
36. Barbara Dennis, *Elizabeth Barrett Browning: The Hope End Years* (Bridgend: Seren, 1996), p.59.
37. Sandra Gilbert, 'From *Patria* to *Matria*: Elizabeth Barrett Browning's Risorgimento', in Joseph Bristow (ed.), *Victorian Women Poets: Emily Brontë, Elizabeth Barrett Browning, Christina Rossetti* (Basingstoke: Macmillan, 1995), pp.132–66.
38. *Aurora Leigh: A Variorum Edition*, ed. Margaret Reynolds (Athens: Ohio University Press, 1992), p.45.
39. See the correspondence with Anna Jameson in *Aurora Leigh* (Norton) ed. Reynolds, pp.340–1.
40. *Ibid.*, p.336.
41. Stone, *Elizabeth Barrett Browning*, p.149.
42. Stephenson, *Elizabeth Barrett Browning*, p.92.
43. Mermin, *Elizabeth Barrett Browning*, p.215.
44. Auguste Comte (1798–1857), French philosopher and founder of sociology, outlined his vision of a positivist society in *Cours de Philosophie Positive* (1830–42) and *Système de Politique Positive* (1851–54). Étienne Cabet (1788–1856), a French-American socialist, founded the Icarian movement and established a utopian society in America based on the principles of pacifism and communism.
45. Stone, *Elizabeth Barrett Browning*, pp.181–2.
46. Barbara Taylor, *Eve and the New Jerusalem: Socialism and Feminism in the Nineteenth Century* (London: Virago, 1983), p.xiv.
47. David, *Intellectual Women*, p.98.
48. Simon Avery and Rebecca Stott, *Elizabeth Barrett Browning* (London: Longman, 2003), p.201.
49. Virginia Woolf, 'Aurora Leigh', in Michèle Barrett (ed.), *Women and Writing* (London: Women's Press, 1979), p.143.

Select Bibliography

WORKS BY EBB

The Battle of Marathon (privately printed, 1820).

An Essay on Mind, with Other Poems (London: James Duncan, 1826).

Prometheus Bound, Translated from the Greek of Æschylus, and Miscellaneous Poems (London: A. J. Valpy, 1833).

The Seraphim, and Other Poems (London: Saunders and Otley, 1838).

Poems, 2 vols (London: Edward Moxon, 1844).

Poems, expanded and revised, 2 vols (London: Chapman and Hall, 1850).

Casa Guidi Windows (London: Chapman and Hall, 1851).

Poems, 4th ed., 3 vols (London: Chapman and Hall, 1856).

Aurora Leigh (London: Chapman and Hall, 1856, with 1857 on title page).

Poems Before Congress (London: Chapman and Hall, 1860).

Last Poems (London: Chapman and Hall, 1862).

The Complete Works of Elizabeth Barrett Browning, ed. Charlotte Porter and Helen A. Clarke, 6 vols (New York: Thomas Y. Cromwell, 1900; reprinted 1973).

Casa Guidi Windows, ed. Julia Markus (Barre, Mass.: Imprint Society, 1977).

Aurora Leigh and Other Poems, ed. Cora Kaplan (London: Women's Press, 1978).

Aurora Leigh: A Variorum Edition, ed. Margaret Reynolds (Athens: Ohio University Press, 1992).

Aurora Leigh, ed. Margaret Reynolds (New York and London: Norton, 1996).

Elizabeth Barrett Browning: Selected Poems, ed. Marjorie Stone and Beverley Taylor (Ontario: Broadview, 2009).

The Works of Elizabeth Barrett Browning, ed. Sandra Donaldson *et al.*, 5 vols (London: Pickering and Chatto, 2010).

CORRESPONDENCE

The Brownings' Correspondence, ed. Philip Kelley, Ronald Hudson and Scott Lewis, 16 vols (Winfield, KS: Wedgestone Press, 1984–).

Robert Browning and Elizabeth Barrett: The Courtship Correspondence 1845–1846, ed. Daniel Karlin (Oxford: Clarendon Press, 1989).

Elizabeth Barrett Browning's Letters to Mrs David Ogilvy, 1849–1861, ed. Peter N. Heydon and Philip Kelley (London: John Murray, 1974).

The Letters of Elizabeth Barrett Browning to Mary Russell Mitford, 1836–1854, ed. Meredith B. Raymond and Mary Rose Sullivan, 3 vols (Winfield, KS: Armstrong Browning Library and Wedgestone Press, 1983).

Florentine Friends: The Letters of Elizabeth Barrett Browning and Robert Browning to Isa Blagden, 1850–1861, ed. Philip Kelley and Sandra Donaldson *et al*. (Waco, TX: Wedgestone Press, 2009).

BIBLIOGRAPHICAL RESOURCE

Donaldson, Sandra, *Elizabeth Barrett Browning: An Annotated Bibliography of the Commentary and Criticism, 1826–1900* (New York: G. K. Hall and Co., 1993).

BIOGRAPHY

Avery, Simon (ed.), *Lives of Victorian Literary Figures: The Brownings* (London: Pickering and Chatto, 2004).

Barrett, R. A., *The Barretts of Jamaica* (Waco, TX: Armstrong Browning Library, 2000).

Dally, Peter, *Elizabeth Barrett Browning: A Psychological Portrait* (London: Macmillan, 1989).

Dennis, Barbara, *Elizabeth Barrett Browning: The Hope End Years* (Bridgend: Seren, 1996).

Forster, Margaret, *Elizabeth Barrett Browning* (London: Chatto and Windus, 1988).

Garrett, Martin, *A Browning Chronology: Elizabeth Barrett and Robert Browning* (Basingstoke: Macmillan, 2000).

———, *Elizabeth Barrett Browning and Robert Browning* (London: The British Library, 2001).

Karlin, Daniel, *The Courtship of Robert Browning and Elizabeth Barrett* (Oxford: Clarendon, 1985).

Marks, Jeannette, *The Family of the Barrett: A Colonial Romance* (New York: Macmillan, 1938).

Markus, Julia, *Dared and Done: The Marriage of Elizabeth Barrett and Robert Browning* (London: Bloomsbury, 1995).

CRITICAL STUDIES

Avery, Simon and Rebecca Stott, *Elizabeth Barrett Browning* (London: Longman, 2003).
Cooper, Helen, *Elizabeth Barrett Browning: Woman and Artist* (Chapel Hill: University of North Carolina Press, 1988).
David, Deirdre, *Intellectual Women and Victorian Patriarchy: Harriet Martineau, Elizabeth Barrett Browning, George Eliot* (London: Macmillan, 1987).
Donaldson, Sandra (ed.), *Critical Essays on Elizabeth Barrett Browning* (New York: G. K. Hall, 1999).
Gridley, Roy, *The Brownings and France* (London: Athlone Press, 1982).
Hayter, Alethea, *Mrs Browning: A Poet's Work and Its Setting* (London: Faber, 1962).
————, *Elizabeth Barrett Browning* (Writers and their Work, London: Longman, 1965).
Leighton, Angela, *Elizabeth Barrett Browning* (Brighton: Harvester Press, 1986).
Lewis, Linda M., *Elizabeth Barrett Browning's Spiritual Progress: Face to Face with God* (Columbia: University of Missouri Press, 1998).
Lootens, Tricia, *Lost Saints: Silence, Gender, and Victorian Literary Canonization* (Charlottesville: University Press of Virginia, 1996).
Mermin, Dorothy, *Elizabeth Barrett Browning: The Origins of a New Poetry* (Chicago: University of Chicago Press, 1989).
Pollock, Mary Sanders, *Elizabeth Barrett Browning and Robert Browning: A Creative Partnership* (Aldershot: Ashgate, 2003).
Radley, Virginia, *Elizabeth Barrett Browning* (Boston: Twayne, 1972).
Stephenson, Glennis, *Elizabeth Barrett Browning and the Poetry of Love* (Ann Arbor, Mich.: U.M.I. Research, 1989).
Stone, Marjorie, *Elizabeth Barrett Browning* (Basingstoke: Macmillan, 1995).

ARTICLES AND BOOK CHAPTERS

Armstrong, Isobel, 'Casa Guidi Windows: Spectacle and Politics in 1851', in Alison Chapman and Jane Stabler (eds), *Unfolding the South: Nineteenth-Century British Women Writers and Artists in Italy*, (Manchester: Manchester University Press, 2003), 51–69.
Avery, Simon, 'Telling It Slant: Promethean, Whig, and Dissenting

Politics in Elizabeth Barrett's Poetry of the 1830s', *Victorian Poetry* 44.4 (2006), 405–424.

———, 'Mapping Political History: Elizabeth Barrett Browning and Nineteenth-Century Historiography', *Victorian Review* 33.2 (2007), 17–33.

———, 'Re-Reading EBB: Trends in Elizabeth Barrett Browning Criticism', *The Journal of Browning Studies* 1 (2010), 5–13.

Battles, Elizabeth, 'Slavery Through the Eyes of a Mother: "The Runaway Slave at Pilgrim's Point"', *Studies in Browning and His Circle* 19 (1991), 93–100.

Blair, Kirstie, *Victorian Poetry and the Culture of the Heart* (Oxford: Clarendon Press, 2006). Chapter on 'EBB and the Woman's Heart'.

Chapman, Alison, 'The Expatriate Poetess: Nationhood, Poetics and Politics', in Alison Chapman (ed.), *Victorian Women Poets* (Cambridge: Brewer, 2003), 57–77.

———, '"In our own blood drenched the pen": Italy and Sensibility in Elizabeth Barrett Browning's *Last Poems'*, *Women's Writing* 10.2 (2003), 269–86.

Cronin, Richard, '*Casa Guidi Windows*: Elizabeth Barrett Browning, Italy and the Poetry of Citizenship', in Alison Chapman and Jane Stabler (eds), *Unfolding the South: Nineteenth-Century British Women Writers and Artists in Italy* (Manchester: Manchester University Press, 2003), pp.35–50.

Dalley, Lana L., 'The least "Angelical" poem in the language: Poetical Economy, Gender, and the Heritage of *Aurora Leigh'*, *Victorian Poetry* 44.4 (2006), 525–42.

Davies, Corinne, 'Two of Elizabeth Barrett Browning's Pan Poems and Their After-Life in Robert Browning's "Pan and Luna"', *Victorian Poetry* 44.4 (2006), 561–70.

Dieleman, Karen, 'Elizabeth Barrett Browning's Religious Poetics: Congregationalist Models of Hymnist and Preacher', *Victorian Poetry* 45.2 (2007), 135–57.

Dillon, Steve, 'Barrett Browning's Poetic Vocation: Crying, Singing, Breathing', *Victorian Poetry* 39.3 (2001), 509–32.

Donaldson, Sandra, '"Motherhood's Advent in Power": Elizabeth Barrett Browning's Poems About Motherhood', *Victorian Poetry* 18.1 (1980), 51–60.

———, 'The Home Front in Elizabeth Barrett Browning's "Mother and Poet" and "The Runaway Slave at Pilgrim's Point"', *Browning Society Notes* 32 (2007), 27–37.

Edmond, Rod, *Affairs of the Hearth: Victorian Narrative Poetry and the Ideology of the Domestic* (London: Routledge, 1988). Chapter on *Aurora Leigh*.

Eisner, Eric, *Nineteenth-Century Poetry and Literary Celebrity* (Basingstoke:

Palgrave Macmillan, 2009). Chapter on 'EBB and the Energies of Fandom'.

Fowler, Rowena, 'On Not Knowing Greek', *The Classical Journal* 78 (1983), 337–49.

Friedman, Susan Stanford, 'Gender and Genre Anxiety: Elizabeth Barrett Browning and H.D. as Epic Poets', *Tulsa Studies in Women's Literature* 5.2 (1986), 203–28.

Gilbert, Sandra, 'From *Patria* to *Matria*: Elizabeth Barrett Browning's *Risorgimento*', in Joseph Bristow (ed.), *Victorian Women Poets* (Basingstoke: Macmillan, 1995), pp.132–66.

Johnson, Stephanie L., '*Aurora Leigh*'s Radical Youth: Derridean *Parergon* and the Narrative Frame in "A Vision of Poets"', *Victorian Poetry* 44.4 (2006), 425–44.

Kaplan, Cora, 'Introduction' to *Aurora Leigh and Other Poems* (London: Women's Press, 1978).

Karlin, Daniel, 'The Discourse of Power in Elizabeth Barrett Browning's Criticism', in Sandra Donaldson (ed.), *Critical Essays on Elizabeth Barrett Browning* (New York: G. K. Hall, 1999), 333–41.

Keirstead, Christopher, 'A Bad Patriot? Elizabeth Barrett Browning and Cosmopolitanism', *Victorians Institute Journal* 33 (2005), 69–95.

Lawson, Kate and Lynn Shakinovsky, *The Marked Body: Domestic Violence in Mid-Nineteenth-Century Literature* (Albany: State University of New York Press, 2002). Chapter on *Aurora Leigh*.

Leighton, Angela, *Victorian Women Poets: Writing Against the Heart* (Hemel Hempstead: Harvester Wheatsheaf, 1992). Chapter on EBB.

Lootens, Tricia, *Lost Saints: Silence, Gender and Victorian Literary Canonization* (Charlottesville: University Press of Virginia, 1996). Chapter on EBB.

Markus, Julia, 'Introduction' to *Casa Guidi Windows* (Barre: Imprint Society, 1977).

Martinez, Michele, 'Sister Arts and Artists: Elizabeth Barrett Browning's *Aurora Leigh* and the Life of Harriet Hosmer', *Forum for Modern Language Studies* 39 (2003), 213–26.

Martens, Britta, '"Hardly shall I tell my joys and sorrows": Robert Browning's Engagement with Elizabeth Barrett Browning's Poetics', *Victorian Poetry* 43.1 (2005), 75–98.

Montwieler, Katherine, 'Domestic Politics: Gender, Protest, and Elizabeth Barrett Browning's *Poems Before Congress*', *Tulsa Studies in Women's Literature* 24.2 (2005), 291–317.

Neri, Barbara, '*Cobridme de flores*: (Un)Covering Flowers of Portuguese and Spanish Poets in *Sonnets from the Portuguese*', *Victorian Poetry* 44.4 (2006), 571–83.

Phelan, Joseph, 'Elizabeth Barrett Browning's *Casa Guidi Windows*, Arthur Hugh Clough's *Amours de Voyage*, and the Italian National

Uprisings of 1847–9', *Journal of Anglo-Italian Studies* 3 (1993), 137–52.

Phelps, Deborah, 'At the Roadside of Humanity: Elizabeth Barrett Browning Abroad', in Michael Cotsell (ed.), *English Literature and the Wider World* vol. 3 (London: Ashfield, 1990).

Reynolds, Matthew, *The Realms of Verse, 1830–1870: English Poetry in a Time of Nation-Building* (Oxford: Oxford University Press, 2001). Chapter on EBB.

Rosenblum, Delores, 'Face to Face: Elizabeth Barrett Browning's *Aurora Leigh* and Nineteenth-Century Poetry', *Victorian Studies* 26 (1983), 321–38.

Stone, Marjorie, 'Cursing as One of the Fine Arts: Elizabeth Barrett Browning's Political Poems', *Dalhousie Review* 66 (1986), 155–73.

——, '*Monna Innominata* and *Sonnets from the Portuguese*: Sonnet Traditions and Spiritual Trajectories', in Mary Arseneau, Antony H. Harrison and Lorraine Janzen Kooistra (eds), *The Culture of Christina Rossetti* (Athens: Ohio University Press, 1999), 46–94.

——, 'Elizabeth Barrett Browning and the Garrisonians: "The Runaway Slave at Pilgrim's Point", the Boston Female Anti-Slavery Society, and Abolitionist Discourse in the *Liberty Bell*' in Alison Chapman (ed.), *Victorian Women Poets* (Cambridge: Brewer, 2003), 33–55.

—— and Beverley Taylor, ' "Confirm my voice": "My sisters", Poetic Audiences, and the Published Voices of EBB', *Victorian Poetry* 44.4 (2006), 391–403.

Taylor, Beverley, 'Elizabeth Barrett Browning and Transnationalism: People Diplomacy in "A Fair-going World"', *Victorian Review* 33.2 (2007), 59–83.

Taylor, Olivia Gatti, 'Written in Blood: The Art of Mothering Epic in the Poetry of Elizabeth Barrett Browning', *Victorian Poetry* 44.2 (2006), 153–64.

Wallace, Anne, ' "Nor in Fading Silks Compose": Sewing, Walking, and Poetic Labour in *Aurora Leigh*', *ELH* 64.1 (1997), 223–56.

Woodworth, Elizabeth, 'Elizabeth Barrett Browning, Coventry Patmore, and Alfred Tennyson on Napoleon III: The Hero-Poet and Carlylean Heroics', *Victorian Poetry* 44.4 (2006), 543–60.

Woolf, Virginia, 'Aurora Leigh', in Michèle Barrett (ed.), *Women and Writing* (London: Women's Press, 1979).

Woolford, John, 'Elizabeth Barrett and the Wordsworthian Sublime', *Essays in Criticism* 45 (1995), 36–56.

Zonana, Joyce, ' "The Embodied Muse": Elizabeth Barrett Browning's *Aurora Leigh* and Feminist Poetics', *Tulsa Studies in Women's Literature* 8.2 (1989), 241–62.

OTHER USEFUL TEXTS

Agulhon, Maurice, *Marianne into Battle: Republican Imagery and Symbolism in France, 1789–1800*, trans. Janet Lloyd (Cambridge: Cambridge University Press, 1981).

Armstrong, Isobel, *Victorian Poetry: Poetry, Poetics, Politics* (London: Routledge, 1993).

————— and Virginia Blain (eds), *Women's Poetry in the Enlightenment: The Making of a Canon, 1730–1820* (Basingstoke: Macmillan, 1999).

————— and Virginia Blain (eds), *Women's Poetry, Late Romantic to Late Victorian: Gender and Genre, 1830–1900* (Basingstoke: Macmillan, 1999).

Bernikow, Louise (ed.), *The World Split Open: Women Poets, 1552–1950* (London: The Women's Press, 1979).

Blain, Virginia (ed.), *Victorian Women Poets: An Annotated Anthology* (Harlow: Longman, 2001).

Bristow, Joseph (ed.), *The Victorian Poet: Poetics and Persona* (London: Croom Helm, 1987).

Chapman, Alison (ed.), *Victorian Women Poets* (Cambridge: Brewer, 2003).

Cronin, Richard, Alison Chapman and Antony H. Harrison (eds), *A Companion to Victorian Poetry* (Oxford: Blackwell, 2002).

Delamotte, Eugenia, *Perils of the Night: Nineteenth-Century Feminist Gothic* (Oxford: Oxford University Press, 1990).

Erkkila, Betsy, *The Wicked Sisters: Women Poets, Literary History, and Discord* (New York and Oxford: Oxford University Press, 1992).

Everett, Susanne, *A History of Slavery* (London: Grange Books, 1997).

Gilbert, Sandra M. and Susan Gubar, *The Madwoman in the Attic: The Woman Writer and the Nineteenth Century Literary Imagination* (New Haven: Yale University Press, 1979).

Guy, Josephine M., *The Victorian Social-Problem Novel: The Market, the Individual and Communal Life* (Basingstoke: Macmillan, 1996).

Harrison, Antony H., *Victorian Poets and Romantic Poems: Intertextuality and Ideology* (Charlottesville: University Press of Virginia, 1990).

—————, *Victorian Poets and the Politics of Culture: Discourse and Ideology* (Charlottesville: University Press of Virginia, 1998).

Jackson, Rosemary, *Fantasy: The Literature of Subversion* (London: Methuen, 1981).

Kaplan, Cora (ed.), *Salt and Bitter and Good: Three Centuries of English and American Women Poets* (London: Paddington Press, 1975).

Knight, Mark and Emma Mason, *Nineteenth-Century Religion and Literature* (Oxford: Oxford University Press, 2006).

Leighton, Angela (ed.), *Victorian Women Poets: A Critical Reader* (Oxford:

Blackwell, 1996).

————— and Margaret Reynolds (eds), *Victorian Women Poets: An Anthology* (Oxford: Blackwell, 1995).

Mason, Emma, *Women Poets of the Nineteenth Century* (Writers and their Work; Tavistock: Northcote House, 2006).

Matthews, Samantha, *Poetical Remains: Poets' Graves, Bodies, and Books in the Nineteenth Century* (Oxford: Oxford University Press, 2004).

McGann, Jerome, *The Romantic Ideology* (Chicago: University of Chicago Press, 1989).

Mellor, Anne K., *Mothers of the Nation: Women's Political Writing in England, 1780–1830* (Bloomington: Indiana University Press, 2000).

Mermin, Dorothy, *Godiva's Ride: Women of Letters in England, 1830–1880* (Bloomington: Indiana University Press, 1993).

Moers, Ellen, *Literary Women* (London: W. H. Allen, 1977).

Neuberger, Julia (ed.), *The Things That Matter: An Anthology of Women's Spiritual Poetry* (London: Kyle Cathie, 1992).

Sinfield, Alan, *Alfred Tennyson* (Oxford: Basil Blackwell, 1986).

Taylor, Barbara, *Eve and the New Jerusalem: Socialism and Feminism in the Nineteenth Century* (London: Virago, 1983).

Wallace, Jennifer, *Shelley and Greece: Rethinking Romantic Hellenism* (Basingstoke: Macmillan, 1997).

Watson, J. R., *English Poetry of the Romantic Period* (London: Longman, 1985).

FICTION

Fish, Laura, *Strange Music* (London: Jonathan Cape, 2008) (novel based on EBB's family written from a Creole and black slave woman's perspective).

Forster, Margaret, *Lady's Maid* (London: Penguin, 1991) (novel of the Brownings' lives told through the perspective of EBB's maid, Lily Wilson).

Woolf, Virginia, *Flush* (London: Hogarth Press, 1933; London: Penguin, 1977) (a 'biography' of EBB through the eyes of her dog).

Index

Mitford, Mary Russell 18, 45
  correspondence with EBB 9,
    19, 59, 64, 72, 73, 80
Moers, Ellen 79
Montwieler, Katherine 24

Napoleon Buonaparte 19, 58–60,
    72, 79
  EBB's poem on 19, 58–60
Neri, Barbara 53
Neuberger, Julia 28
Newman, John Henry 30
New Monthly Magazine 12
Newton, Isaac 3
Nightingale, Florence, *Cassandra*
    105n.
North American Review 14

Odyssey 88
Ogilvy, Eliza 22, 40
Oxford Movement 30

Paine, Thomas 3
Petrarch 3
Phelan, Joseph 53, 104n., 108n.
Philhellenism: see Greek politics/
  Greek War of Independence
Pindar 4
Plath, Sylvia, 'Cut' 65
Plato 3
Pliny 4
Politics: see entries for American
  politics; French politics; Greek
  politics; Italian politics
Poet Laureate, EBB proposed as
  1
poetics, EBB's 1–26 and *passim.*
Pollock, Mary Sanders 21, 74
Pope, Alexander 3
Price, Uvedale 4
Pulham, Patricia 106n.

Racine, Jean 3
Radcliffe, Ann 106n.

Radley, Virginia 45
religion
  Anglicanism 28, 29, 30
  Congregationalism: see
    separate entry
  EBB's knowledge of religious
    debates 29
  EBB's religious poetics 16–17,
    27–39
  EBB's religious reading 29
  Evangelical revivals 28
  Higher Criticism of the Bible
    30
  Oxford Movement 30
  and science 30
*Report of the Royal Commission on
  the Employment of Children* 60
Reynolds, Margaret xvii, 88, 93,
    106n.
Reynolds, Matthew 77, 108n.
Richardson, Alan 63
Romantic poets 4–11, 20, 22, 37
Rossetti, Christina 21, 27, 38, 42
  Goblin Market xvii, 87, 105n.
Rossetti, Dante Gabriel 21, 42
  'Jenny' 87

Sage, Lorna xvii
Sallust 4
Sand, George 20–1, 59, 88
Sappho 20
Scott, Walter 42
Scully, James 15
Shakespeare, William 3
Shakinovsky, Lynn 89
Shelley, Percy Bysshe 10–11, 15,
    37
  A Defence of Poetry 11
  Alastor 5
Sinfield, Alan 6, 79
slavery 23, 63–8, 100
Smith, Barbara Leigh, *Women and
  Work* 81
sonnet sequence: see *Works:*